Solving The
SENIOR
HOUSING
PUZZLE

Family Guide to Choosing the Right Options for Mom or Dad

To

From

Gene Guarino

Solving The Senior Housing Puzzle: Family Guide to Choosing the Right Options for Mom or Dad

© 2020 by Savior Publishing House LLC
2140 Hall Johnson Ste. 102-320
Grapevine, TX 76051
info@saviorpublishinghouse.com
817-502-9478

ISBN: 978-1-7351089-1-9

Savior Publishing House LLC is a national publisher that partners with local experts in real estate who have a desire to serve their clients before themselves; in this sense, we only work with the leading experts in a given area.

If you find value in this and other books, please pass them on to people you know, like, and trust. Our company's mission is to help over 1,000,000 seniors and their adult children formulate the best possible plan. Thanks to a great network of local experts, we will continue to make a difference through knowledge and education.

Disclaimer

The content of this book is intended for general informational and educational purposes only. The information in this book is not meant to replace the advice of a certified professional. Please consult a licensed advisor in matters relating to your personal and professional wellbeing, including your mental, emotional and physical health, finances, business, legal matters, and education. The views and opinions expressed throughout the book are those of the author and do not necessarily reflect the views or opinions of any other agency, organization, employer, publisher, or company. Since we are critically thinking human beings, the views of the author are always subject to change at any time. No warranties or guarantees are expressed or implied by the publisher's choice to include any of the content in this volume.

If you choose to attempt any of the methods mentioned in this book, the author and publisher advise you to take full responsibility for your results. The author and publisher are not liable for any damages or negative consequences from any treatment, action, application, or preparation to any person reading or following the information in this book.

Table of Contents

Dedication

This book is dedicated to my amazing wife, Mona.

After a mere 35 years of marriage, four incredible kids, and two wonderful grandkids, we are just getting started.

Thank you for your support, your love, and your light.

It is truly an honor and a blessing to take this journey we call life with you.

I love you,
Gene

FOREWORD

Hi. My name is Max Keller, and I am excited that you picked up a copy of this valuable resource. I have been involved in helping seniors for more than two decades and have been educating seniors on their real estate options since 2015. Since I met Gene Guarino, I have seen him and his organization directly and indirectly impact thousands of seniors and their families.

Before getting into real estate full time, I was personally in charge of helping my grandmother (best friend) navigate the challenges of staying in her home, helping her with finances, and managing her declining health and mobility. My grandmother helped take care of me for the first fifteen years of my life, and I helped take care of her for the last fifteen years of her life. I wish this book had been available when I was helping her because it was challenging to find the right professional who could answer my questions objectively. There is so much to learn when a loved one gets older and needs extra help. Not only did I struggle to find accurate answers to my questions, but I also did not know all the questions I needed to be asking.

Gene has done an excellent job in this book to simplify the journey families embark on as they figure out the types of senior housing options available, the cost, how to pay for care, and how to sell or keep an existing home. This book can serve as the reference guide for you and your family as you go through the same journey I did. If you want to gain the knowledge needed to make the best decisions, help your senior enjoy their final years, and have as little stress as possible, this book will help you.

I was a teacher for seven years before I got into real estate full time. Some people just have the heart of a teacher, and Gene is one of those people. This book summarizes many of the principals and strategies Gene has taught to his students, association members, and community. His teaching conversations with thousands of his students are echoed in this easy-to-understand guide.

Education is power, and this book will empower any family who reads it with the knowledge and tools needed to create a better outcome for their loved ones. Unfortunately, too many people avoid talking about this topic, fail to plan, and end up in panic mode when a family member has a health crisis. Planning ahead and following the steps outlined in this book will help your team create the best outcome possible for your family.

For most seniors, multiple people will help them develop their housing plan. In this book, Gene will advise you who should be involved in the planning process and how to find the right person to work with. Read this guide with your family. As you and your family member(s) discuss the senior housing options available to you, I hope that the information provided herein will shine a light on the best choices.

Gene and his community specialize in providing high-quality care to residents, informing current and prospective families of their options, and providing a network of trusted referral partners.

I hope you share *Solving the Senior Housing Puzzle* with your friends and co-workers and get clarity on your senior housing plan. – Max Keller

BUILDING YOUR ROADMAP

Solving the senior housing puzzle is very simple: the more you plan, the better the outcome will be.

Planning ahead is the key, but how do you start?

Dave Ramsey, the famous financial planner, recommends obtaining long-term care insurance at age 60. (We discuss long-term care insurance in a later chapter.) We recommend that you start your Senior Housing Plan—for yourself or your loved one—at or before age 60.

According to the Centers for Disease Control and Prevention, life expectancy is currently 78.8 years.[1] Putting a plan in place 18 years in advance can smooth out some of the speed bumps that life may put in our way.

It is essential to map out exactly where you or your senior want to be as you transition into senior housing. The type of lifestyle you envision having and the services you need to access will significantly influence your ideal destination.

A TALE OF TWO ROADMAPS

OPTION ONE – NORMAL PACE

Perhaps everything is going well now, and you are in the planning phase. Maybe you picked this book up early and decided that this roadmap is too important to leave to chance. During this planning stage, you will figure out what your goals, dreams, and desires are. It is time to determine what type of housing is the right fit and run through some "what if" scenarios to test your plan. For example:

- If your spouse dies, where do you want to live?

- If you get sick or fall and injure yourself, will you move in with a family member or continue living alone?

If you or your senior were to become ill or injured and require extra medical care, what would the ideal outcome be for you? Have this conversation with your family right now.

If you are the child of a senior, read this book with your parent and say, "Mom/Dad, if you were to need extra care, would you want to live with us? We would love to have you living with us. You would not be a burden, and we would take care of you. We love you!"

Alternatively, you could say the opposite: "Mom/Dad, we love you, but we are not equipped to take care of you. If x, y, or z happens, where would you want to live?"

Another great question could be, "Mom/Dad, if you needed some extra care, where would you want to live? Would you want to live close to church? Would you want to be close to us?"

If your senior needs new housing options, would they stay in the city or state where they have their local network, or move across town, state, or even country to be somewhere closer to their adult children? There are no right or wrong answers, but you need to know the answers to these questions before an issue arises. Please do not assume a senior will want to move or stay where they currently live. Discuss this ahead of time and determine the ideal destination and situation if extra care is needed.

OPTION TWO – FAST-TRACK PACE

Something unexpected has happened, and you need to make a senior housing switch immediately. What do you do now?

Our goal is to make this difficult time easier for you. You can read this book from start to finish, or you can fast forward to the information you need right now.

Use the checklists in this book to assist you in building your roadmap. Although something may have happened necessitating a change in your senior's housing situation—and there may not be a plan to navigate it—there is an ideal destination.

You may not be able to put a perfect plan together quickly, but we are confident that if you use the information in these chapters, you can put an excellent plan together depending on your family's needs and what is important to you.

In most cases, multiple people help a senior develop their housing plan. In this book, we will address the senior's needs and a caring family member's or friend's needs.

This book can benefit families going through a health crisis and are overwhelmed with the many options or who are already in the senior housing planning stages.

Read this guide with your family. As you and your family member(s) discuss the senior housing options available to you, I hope that the information provided herein will shine a light on the best choices.

LIMITATIONS

It would be difficult to cover every option for every situation. Some areas of your roadmap will require the help of an attorney, financial planner, or other professional. It would be a disservice to you for us to claim to be all things to all people. We specialize in providing high-quality care to our residents, informing our current and prospective families of their options, and helping you access our network of referral partners.

PLANNING CHECKLIST

If you are working together with an adult child to make these decisions, each of you will need to answer the questions below. Combine your answers to determine the ideal situation.

FAST-TRACK CHECKLIST

- ❏ What type of facility do you want to be in?
- ❏ What type of care is necessary based on medical facts?
- ❏ What amenities are important to you?
- ❏ What geographical location do you want to stay in?
- ❏ What is your monthly budget?
- ❏ How long will your resources last?
- ❏ What are your current mobility needs, and how will that affect the choice of where to live next?
- ❏ Should you sell your house or keep it?
- ❏ What are the pros and cons of aging in place at home?

2
SENIOR HOUSING OPTIONS

In this chapter, we'll address the following questions:

- How do you select a senior living facility before you need to be in one?

- What will it take for you and your family to be happy with a senior housing facility?

- Can this facility grow with you if you require additional care, or will you need to move to a different facility?

There is a wide range of options, services, and prices for senior housing. Make sure you understand what is included and what is not (extras) when you are looking for a new residence. Think about what type of care you need now and what type of care you may need in the future.

Hopefully, you are looking at senior living facilities before you need to be in one. If there has been a recent and sudden health change, you may not have the luxury of time.

RIGHT IDEA, WRONG PLAN

Margo never told her adult children, James and Mary, that she had been falling at home. When James took his mom to the doctor, the doctor noticed that there were marks on Margo's shoulder and hip. Margo said she had scraped up against a shrub and bumped into the wall, but the doctor knew something was not quite right. He questioned her story and eventually, Margo came clean.

The fact is Margo needed help. She didn't want to tell her kids and cause them stress, knowing she needed more help than her busy family could provide. They all felt bad, but the good news is there were options available to her.

Margo's family worked on a Senior Housing Plan to allow her to get more care and feel more secure. Margo had some mobility issues, but she had been taking her medicine, cooking for herself, and even doing her own chores.

The family tried to do their best, but they did not understand the various senior housing choices. They put Margo in a facility with many wonderful services, most of which she did not need, however, such as medication assistance, food preparation, and laundry services, amongst other activities.

Unfortunately, Margo was now paying almost double what she would have been paying if she was in a facility that better met her needs. Even though the facility was great, the level of care was too high for Margo's needs, and the enormous monthly bill created a financial strain on the family.

An unexpected side effect of Margo living at the new facility with all of its services was that she no longer did things for herself. She became more dependent on others, and she lost her independence little by little in the process, which could have been avoided if the family had more information about the options available for Margo.

BENEFITS OF PLANNING EARLY

If you're planning ahead, use this information to determine what services are required and find a couple of facilities that meet your needs. There are many benefits to planning for senior housing before it's needed. You and your family will have peace of mind knowing you are prepared.

VACANCY

The best cost-to-value facilities in our area fill up quickly, and it can be challenging to secure a spot. A client called one of our offices saying that she needed to quickly sell her home because an apartment had opened up at a facility where she had been on the waiting list for over 12 months.

The facility required her to put a deposit down and quickly decide before they moved on to the next name on the list.

If you wait until the last minute to make a senior housing choice, you may end up paying more than you had budgeted or living somewhere you do not like.

SUPPLY AND DEMAND

Senior housing is typically more expensive than people realize, and high-quality places can fill up fast, so you want to have these places on your shortlist and figure out how far in advance you need to reserve a spot.

In many parts of the country, new senior housing facilities are being built all the time. There is more supply in many cities than demand, but as more seniors reach retirement age and new seniors move into those areas, that could shift.

INFORMATION OVERLOAD

Blogs, online reviews, websites, and online advertisements intended to create clarity often result in information overload. Not all of the information online about senior housing is true or objective. An online article about senior housing may, in fact, be a clever sales letter.

Some clients start their research online, but after reading several "Top 5" articles and looking at reviews on websites, they are more confused and are no closer to making a senior housing decision.

Pricing for senior housing is rarely disclosed online or over the phone. Each facility is unique, so it isn't easy to compare one facility to another.

By the end of this chapter, we hope that you will be able to map out what is important to you, know how to locate facilities, and be able to choose the right one. In the next chapter, we will give you information about the costs at the different facilities.

PICTURE PERFECT

Imagine having a Senior Housing Plan prepared in advance that you can hand to a family member if needed. This plan would break down the three major categories of senior living facilities with one or two places pre-screened and selected.

Because you were not in a rush, you had ample time to pick the senior housing facility with the right mix of values, staff excellence, service, and price. However, if there has been a recent loss of mobility or memory, or more medical care is required than you can manage by yourself, use the information and checklists in this chapter to identify the level of care needed and start your search today.

Right Facility at the Right Time

In the following sections, we will outline three of the most popular senior housing choices—independent living, assisted living, and nursing care. We will do our best to give you the pros and cons of each option objectively.

Independent Living

Age-Restricted Communities

Age-restricted communities can be apartments, single-family homes, garden homes, and even townhouses. These communities have a "connected" feel and attract seniors who want access to activities ranging from arts and crafts and bingo to a gym and a swimming pool. Some facilities with higher-end amenities may add golf or tennis.

This type of facility is typically geared towards independent seniors who could live alone in their own houses but want to socialize with other people their age. They are also looking for less home and yard maintenance than if they lived on their own.

Most independent living age-restricted communities do not allow people under 55 years old to live there. If your adult child currently lives with you and you are considering moving to an age-restricted community, be sure to check with that community to make sure that this would be possible.

One of our partner companies bought a home from a couple who were moving to a 55+ community. The house was beautiful, but the couple wanted a place that required less maintenance. Living in an apartment, they could work their regular jobs and go camping in their towable camper on weekends and holidays.

SENIOR APARTMENTS, TOWNHOUSES, AND GARDEN HOMES

These types of senior housing are similar to the age-restricted communities but usually have fewer amenities and are less expensive, making them an excellent option for folks who are downsizing but still want privacy.

Some of these senior communities have a percentage of units available to lower-income seniors that qualify. Also, these communities may have a gated entrance and ADA-compliant units. They can be a great opportunity for someone who does not desire as much socialization but still wants to live in a community of seniors.

MOVE IN WITH A FAMILY MEMBER

As you can imagine, there are many pros and cons to this option. Living with a family member is becoming a popular choice for many reasons, one of which is financial. Although there is competition among senior housing providers, most senior housing is more expensive than the average home mortgage.

All senior housing is more expensive than living with a family member. If something does not go according to plan or there is no plan, living with a family member can be one of your only options. It can also strain even the best family relationships. You should count the cost beyond just the financial cost. Living with family can be a good or bad idea, depending on the family dynamics. If you have a strained relationship with your family, they may not be amenable to you moving in with them. On the other hand, if your relationship is really great, having you move in may not be a burden.

Some clients have their parent(s) move in for health and safety reasons, or so that the grandparent(s) can be at home when the grandkids get home from school.

For this arrangement to work, everyone needs to be on the same page, which goes back to planning. We have met families where the husband feels great about their parent(s) moving in, but the wife or grandkids do not.

Start this conversation today (if you have not already). If my kids do not want to take me in, I would rather find out now —while I still have time to create a plan B—than have them resent me when my physical condition is poor.

Ask your spouse or family this simple question: "If my mom (or dad) needs to leave her (his) home, can she (he) move in with us? Why or why not?"

If you are a senior who is considering moving in with your kids or a family member, ask them what they think about the idea. The best way to get an honest answer is to ask a "yes" or "no" question and tell them whatever answer they give is acceptable.

If you move into a family member's home, learn the house rules. Get some space and privacy for yourself. Having a room or quiet place to be alone will help everyone. Set boundaries in advance. For example, "After 7 pm, I like to have some time by myself to think."

We worked with a senior couple who sold their house, and their adult son sold his house at the same time. They pooled their resources to buy some land with two houses, one for each family. If the porch light was on, that meant they were accepting visitors (grandkids and other family members). If the porch light was off, they needed alone time. That sounds like it could be fun if you get along with your family.

Renting a Room

Many seniors will rent out a room in their home to help cover expenses and create a sense of community. Usually, tenants that live with seniors will help them around the house in exchange for free or reduced rent. Some may be skeptical of this arrangement after hearing random stories from others who have allowed strangers to live in their homes.

Other seniors may rent a room in a home to save money on housing costs, such as maintenance, insurance, taxes, etc.

We do not recommend either of these options unless you really know the person you will be living with, and you should get a full background check and always trust your instincts.

If there is a situation where three people have been best friends for 30 years, and they are all widows in their 80s, that might work. However, they would each need their own space and should set ground rules for the home.

Set up personal boundaries. It is a lot easier to be friends with somebody you see occasionally for two to three hours at a time than to live with them.

ASSISTED LIVING

Before we discuss your assisted living options, let's understand who assisted living is really for.

AARP did a survey and asked its members, "Would you rather stay at home or move into an assisted living facility if you needed help with your Activities of Daily Living?" The response was exactly what you would expect. 90% of members who responded said they would rather stay at home and get the help they needed. Unfortunately, 70% of us will need assistance with our ADLs for an average of 3.5 years during our lifetimes, and those are who Assisted Living is designed to help. No one moves into Assisted Living unless they need assistance. Those that can afford to may move in earlier when their level of care is lower. But remember, it's not a vacation home or a "retirement" community with pickleball, golf, and tennis. It is for people that need assistance but do not need daily nursing care. The challenge for many of us is we may not recognize that need for ourselves, and we may not want to admit it if we do.

LARGE CORPORATE LOCATIONS

Assisted living facilities can give you access to a broad range of services, from help with basic personal care, such as getting dressed, taking medicine, and bathing, to more advanced assistance. Assisted living facilities can feel like living in a hotel, and most facilities are fully furnished. If you enjoy staying in hotels and having lots of people around, this option could appeal to you.

Some facilities have sections with independent, apartment-style rooms and a separate area that focuses more on hands-on care. Services at these facilities can include meals, daily activities, transportation, and security.

If a senior is starting to have memory problems but can still live independently, they may live in an assisted living facility with adequately trained staff and appropriate safety features. If the senior needs more advanced memory services, those are handled in a special care unit that usually falls under skilled nursing care.[2]

You can choose from national brands or local non-chain facilities. Look at each location on a facility-by-facility basis before making your selection. Your decision will come down to the mix of people living and working there and the price for the value that you are getting. A great management team is a must-have.

QUESTIONS TO CONSIDER

- How close is the facility?
- Can the kids and grandkids easily visit?
- How do the managers interact with staff and residents?
- Does it feel like a "team" or is there obvious stress amongst the staff?
- How long has the management team been in place?
- How do the workers interact with the residents and with each other?

At most of the facilities we visit, the managers and workers want to be there.

RESIDENTIAL ASSISTED LIVING HOMES

With the recent health concerns surrounding the COVID-19 pandemic, especially in nursing homes, Residential Assisted Living (RAL) homes are becoming more popular every day.

There are more than 29,000 RAL homes across the country today. They're not as easy to find as large nursing home facilities since they aren't built on 10 acres of land along a busy road with a sign in the front. Typically, there will be five to 15 residents in each home, and residents can choose private rooms with private baths or shared rooms with shared baths. Unlike larger Assisted Living communities, RAL home charges usually cover all costs so there are no surprises. RAL homes have a "family" feel and not a big institutional feel.

RAL homes with ten or more residents are usually larger homes (4,000+ sq ft) in nice neighborhoods. There's enough room for the residents to have private space with the option of being active and involved in a smaller community. It's the best of both worlds for many reasons. It's not a hotel trying to *feel* like home but an actual *home* in a residential neighborhood.

With fewer residents and visitors, there are not as many opportunities to spread germs. It is becoming more important to ensure anyone in assisted living is well cared for and safe.

These homes offer many of the same services as larger assisted living communities. One of our clients who moved into a RAL home was able to stay in a neighborhood similar to where she previously lived. She told us that her favorite aspects of the home were the friendships with the residents and the large back porch and yard.

RAL properties attract residents who like the idea of being in a home, sharing a meal with a small group of people, relaxing in the backyard, and feeling like they are still in their old homes. Most RAL homes have a staff member who arrives in the morning, someone who comes in the evening and stays overnight, and an on-call nurse. The management team is often led by individuals who worked at larger facilities but preferred to be at a smaller location. Many of these RAL homes have services to provide meals for the residents.

Before you consider moving into an Assisted Living community, large or small, make sure you know the ratio of "direct caregiving staff" to residents. Larger facilities with 100 or 200 beds may claim to have a 10:1 ratio. But, when you take out the landscaper, kitchen help, administrative staff, and management, that ratio may be closer to 20:1. At night, it could be 50+:1.

In a RAL home, the care is much more personal.

States typically do not require a specific ratio within a community, large or small. They leave it up to the owner. Many times, those decisions are driven by the financial effect they produce. In a typical RAL home, the resident to direct care staff may be closer to 5 or 6 to one, which also represents the biggest cost for the business. The RAL home spends most of their budget on great caregivers rather than maintaining large buildings and properties.

QUESTIONS TO CONSIDER

Would you rather live in a large community with 200 residents or a residential home in a neighborhood?

Would you rather live somewhere that has a 5:1 or 20:1 caregiver to resident ratio?

With a 20:1 ratio, you may not get the attention you need. The caregivers would not be able to spend enough time with you even if they wanted to.

How close are you to your kids?

If they are within 20 minutes, they will likely visit more often. Maybe that's good, or maybe that's not so good. If it's easy to come and see you without being required to make an appointment, they will be more spontaneous and drop by when they can. If it's easy to park and walk in the front door to see me instead of parking in a large lot and walking a long distance to the entrance, which would I choose?

I'd rather see my kids twice a week for an hour then once a month for an afternoon.

TO FIND A RAL HOME NEAR YOU VISIT
HTTPS://RALNA.ORG/FIND-A-HOME/

MEMORY CARE FACILITIES

Memory care facilities, or special care units (SPUs), are specifically for patients with Alzheimer's or other forms of dementia. These units are specially designed to protect patients from getting lost. Treatment options are available to address behavioral needs since Alzheimer's and other forms of dementia evolve with each stage.[3]

The staff at memory care facilities are skilled at identifying changes in these stages and adjusting the patient's treatment plan accordingly. Patients are encouraged to live as independently as possible.

The benefits of memory care facilities include fewer patient falls and hospital visits, and a more consistent administering of medicine than if a resident lives at home in a confused state.

Although these facilities may be in a separate area of an assisted living facility, the residents interact with other community members and are not isolated.

NURSING HOMES

Skilled nursing facilities (SNF) are for individuals who require skilled medical care. These facilities have Registered Nurses (RNs) on staff 24/7. They may also have licensed practical nurses (LPNs) and licensed vocational nurses (LVNs).[4] Care at these facilities can include:

- Personal care (housekeeping, laundry, meals, bathing)
- Monitoring medical signs
- Managing a patient's care plan
- Observing a patient's conditions
- Tube feedings
- Rehabilitation services
- Therapeutic exercises or activities
- Dental services
- Recreational activities

Treatments are provided by skilled staff and other specialists, such as occupational therapists and speech therapists, who come to the facility to treat patients.[5] Not all services are available at every facility, so make sure you know what each facility offers. Examples of specialized care include:

- Rehabilitative therapy
- Dialysis
- Working with Alzheimer's and dementia patients
- IV drug therapy

Continuing Care Retirement Communities (CCRC)

A CCRC is a hybrid since it can fit into all three categories. To be classified as a CCRC (life-plan community), a community must offer independent living, assisted living, and skilled nursing care all in the same facility or campus.

If you are a senior, you must move into a CCRC when you are healthy and live independently. Communities consist of houses, townhouses, or apartments, while the amenities available can be resort level, frequently including golf, tennis, and other higher-end amenities.[6] CCRCs generally have an ownership option, which we will discuss in the next chapter. If your budget is not limited, you are looking for a resort-style retirement, and you like the idea of having more services available as you need them without having to move, look into a CCRC.[7]

Finding Your Ideal Facility

Hopefully, the content that we have covered so far will get you and your team into the right mindset to find a facility.

Needs and Wants

Identify your current needs, forecast your possible future needs, and identify your wants or "wish list." Price is important, but do not let it be the sole determining factor in your decision.

When calling local facilities to ask how much they charge, most will tell you, "It depends on what you want or need."

Pricing is more complicated than booking a hotel room. Determine your needs, preferences, and have a basic idea of your budget—then see where the process leads you. Answer each one of the following questions with your team.

YOUR PLAN CHECKLIST

- ❑ Are you currently facing any problems or challenges?
- ❑ What is the biggest problem you are trying to solve?
- ❑ How soon do you expect to move into a senior facility?
- ❑ In what geographical location do you want to live?
- ❑ Do you have a specific housing need right now? If so, what is it (e.g., independent, assisted, nursing, specialty)?
- ❑ What prompted you to start this search?
- ❑ Where do you currently live?
- ❑ How long will it take to sell your home and/or move?
- ❑ Who are the members of your advisory team (e.g., spouse, children, family members, religious leader, medical team, or professionals)?
- ❑ Is your advisory team part of your planning process?
- ❑ If price were not a factor, where would you want to live?
- ❑ In which type of environment do you want to live (e.g., private, community, social, private room, shared room, private house, or first floor)?
- ❑ What amenities would you like to have available (e.g., entertainment, recreation, food, pool, classes, and transportation)?
- ❑ What personal care services do you need now or want to be available (e.g., dressing, mobility help, laundry, bathing, and food)?
- ❑ What medical care services do you need now or want to be available (e.g., treatments, specialty care, medicine, and diabetes care)?

Your Team Checklist

❑ Do you have the following professionals on your team? If so, list them below:

    ❑ Attorney

    ❑ Financial advisor

    ❑ CPA

    ❑ Medical doctor

    ❑ Family members and other advisors

❑ Are there any other needs or wants you have that are important to you but have not yet been mentioned?

❑ What is important to the members of your advisory team? Ask them if you have not already. For example, "I am creating a Senior Housing Plan that I expect to begin following (next month, next year, or in ten years). What is important to you?"

❑ Ask your advisory team, "Is there anything else you want me to consider as I am creating my plan"?

Your Closest Advisor Checklist

❑ Do you have any concerns regarding my health, safety, and overall happiness?

❑ What challenges are you facing as my top advisor?

❑ Is moving in with you or a family member an option?

OTHER PLANNING QUESTIONS

❏ Are you married?

❏ Do you currently live with anyone else?

❏ If you move, where will your current house partner (e.g., friend, family, or spouse) live?

❏ If your spouse were to die before you, would you want to stay in your current home?

❏ Would you prefer to move into a facility that has all the care options available—from independent to nursing—or would you be fine moving to a new facility if you needed more care?

❏ Do you want to be close to a place of worship?

❏ Is there a friend or family member you want to live near?

❏ If you are considering moving across the city, state, or country, will you need to find a new doctor or other professionals?

❏ If you are moving into a furnished facility, what is the plan for your current furniture and personal belongings?

❏ If you plan to give items from your home away to family members, have you let them know?

❏ Will you get input from your family members before you give them any of your personal belongings?

❏ When you give a family member or friend your personal belongings, is it for them to keep or are you just asking them to store the items for you?

❏ Will you need to rent a storage facility? If so, where?

❏ How will you know when it is time to make a decision?

Your Budget Checklist

❏ Do you use a monthly budget?

❏ What monthly amount can you afford for senior housing and care expenses?

❏ What financial sources are available to pay for housing?

❏ If you do not need senior housing right now, have you inquired about long-term care insurance?

❏ Do you expect family members to help pay for your housing? If so, how much do they plan to contribute?

❏ If you plan to sell your home, how much do you expect to receive?

Identify and Interview

Once you map out what is important to you and your team and know what you want and need and how much you have available from your budget, you can start identifying and interviewing facilities. You can find facilities online, from print media, through referrals from friends, or by contacting local or national referral services.

Answer the questions below at each step of the process. After you narrow down your choices, visit a minimum of three to four facilities for each type of care you may require. Carry a checklist to complete for each facility so that you can evaluate and compare them.

BEFORE YOU CALL (IDENTIFY)

❏ How did I find out about this facility?

❏ How many of my needs does this facility meet?

❏ How many of my wants does this facility meet?

❏ Does this facility have the level of care I may need in the future?

❏ What do the online reviews say about this facility? (See Google, Facebook, and the Better Business Bureau).

CALL THE FACILITY (PHONE INTERVIEW)

❏ Do you have any openings at your facility?

❏ What services do you provide?

❏ Do you perform background checks on your staff? What about the residents?

❏ Is your facility accredited? If so, with who?

❏ How much should I budget if I move into your facility (not an exact number, just a range)?

❏ If I become a resident, how often do rates change?

❏ What is the best way I can get more information about your facility?

❏ When can I take a tour of the facility and learn more?

QUESTIONS FOR THE TOUR (IN-PERSON INTERVIEW)

- ❏ Ask your tour guide how long they have worked there and what their main focus is.

- ❏ Who is the current manager or director? How long have they been there?

- ❏ What services are not offered here?

- ❏ What do you like about working here?

- ❏ What would you change about the facility if you could?

- ❏ Ask if you can speak to other employees and residents about their experiences at the facility.

- ❏ How do you communicate with family members?

- ❏ When are the visiting hours?

- ❏ Do they have any referrals of current residents or past residents/family members that you can contact?

- ❏ Is this a for-profit or non-profit facility? If you have experience with each one, what differences do you see?

- ❏ If I were to move in today and order certain services, what would the cost be?

- ❏ How often do rates change for residents?

- ❏ How often do rates change for the general public (non-residents)?

- ❏ Is the rate open to negotiation? If so, under what circumstances?

- ❏ What is the application process? How long does it take?

- ❏ Are there other questions I should have asked?

- ❏ How long can we take to decide?

MAKING A DECISION

After you complete your interviews and tours, sit down with your team and narrow down the list to your top two choices. If you need to move quickly, call the facility at the top of your list and start the application process. If your top facility is not available when you need it, you can choose the alternative.

If moving into a senior housing facility is not in your immediate future, having a couple of choices in each of the three areas will significantly reduce the time needed to resume the search when making a choice becomes urgent.

THINGS THAT CAN GO WRONG

THE FACILITY YOU CHOSE IS FULL

If the facility you want is fully booked, get on the waiting list, so when you are ready to move in 6 or 12 months, there should be an opening. If you are serious about moving into a certain facility, you may be required to put down a small deposit.

SELECTING THE WRONG LEVEL OF CARE

Selecting a facility that has the wrong level of care can be an expensive mistake. All of the extra services can seem inexpensive when priced individually, but together they can be a budget-buster—you want to live somewhere you can afford.

If cost is a concern, make sure you are only receiving the services you need. You do not want to live in a facility for three or six months and find out you can no longer afford to live there. Getting an accurate estimate of all costs and potential increases before you move in will help you mitigate this risk.

NOT PROPERLY BUDGETING

Set your monthly budget and plan for all your expenses, not only for your senior housing. The sooner you understand the costs of senior living and can begin to save and budget for them, the more successful you will be.

Build out your plan and expect to pay more than you have ever paid for housing and other services. In the next chapter, we will review some typical costs. Confirm these costs when you go on facility tours so you will have the information you need to get your budget ready.

NEXT STEPS

The decision to plan is yours, and the time to begin the plan is today. Deciding to move depends on what you or your team determine. Hopefully, we have given you some new ideas and information that will help. We hope that the checklists in this book will help you organize your process to get results faster.

CHAPTER GOAL

The goal of this chapter was to review some of the most popular senior housing choices and facilitate a discussion between you and your senior housing team.

If you have answered all the questions and completed the steps in this chapter, you know more about senior housing than 99% of your peers. If you know a senior or a senior's family member who could also use this information, contact us so we can get this book to them.

3
SENIOR HOUSING COSTS

Nursing home care is expensive—sometimes as much as $7,200 a month. How much money do you have available each month to pay for senior housing, and will it be enough?

Many seniors sell their homes to use the proceeds to pay for senior housing. What happens when that money runs out? Are there family members willing and able to move the senior into their home?

Hopefully, the tips in this chapter will help you prepare.

COSTS AND AFFORDABILITY

It is difficult to precisely determine the costs for senior housing because there are so many variables. We will share some average ranges that we see in many parts of the country (at the time of publishing this book). These numbers will give you a starting point. Use the tools in the previous chapter to get the exact numbers for your area. Good luck!

INDEPENDENT CARE

Independent care housing can cost less than $1,000 per month (for a small gated apartment with few amenities) to more than $4,000 per month (for a higher-end planned community). Most facilities with a large list of amenities and services will have a base rate of $2,000 to $3,000 per month. Other services or memberships are available at an additional cost if desired.[8]

Keep in mind that there are deals to be found in any market. If you are flexible about location and amenities and have time to do an extensive search, you find housing that costs half of what is listed above.

If you still have a mortgage on your house, remember that the money you use to pay your mortgage, along with taxes and maintenance on your current home, will now go towards your new housing. When you factor that in, a facility in the price range above may not be that much more than what you are currently paying.

Most independent living facilities have been retrofitted to accommodate people with mobility issues. If you plan to invest $5,000 or $10,000 to make changes to your current home, you can use that money to pay the fees for your new facility instead.

ASSISTED LIVING FACILITIES

According to the Genworth Financial Cost of Care Survey recently released by Genworth Financial Inc. of Richmond, the national median monthly rate for a private room in an assisted living facility is $4,051.[9]

According to a report by Acclaro Growth Partners, the average stay in an assisted living facility is 29 months.

So, if you multiply $4,051 by 29 months, the cost is well over the national average of $100,000. In some areas of the country, that amount can be twice as much or more.

NURSING CARE FACILITIES

According to the American Health Care Association (*www.ahcancal.org*), 59% of assisted living residents eventually move to a skilled nursing facility. The average stay in a nursing home is one to three years.[10]

In many parts of the country, nursing home prices can be $7,000 per month and higher. If you put all these costs together —and consider that, on average, you are looking at about four to five years of some type of long-term care—you can easily spend over $200,000. This estimate does not include any doctor or hospital bills that a senior may incur during that period.

CONTINUING CARE RETIREMENT COMMUNITIES (CCRC)

Entry fees to live in a home or condo in a planned community can range from low- to mid-six figures depending on your location. Monthly charges range from $2,000 to more than $4000 per month.[11]

These facilities have Life Care (Type A) contracts that will cover all required care at the facility, even if the level of care increases. Since the facility is taking on more risk, residents are required to pay a large down payment.

Type B contracts allow residents to pay for care at discounted rates when needed with a smaller down payment than required by a Type A contract. If you have a long-term care policy that covers your extra care costs, you can select a Type C contract that will charge you the going rate when care is needed.

If the resident dies within a few years of moving in, a declining portion of the entry fee is refunded. Some people pay the CCRC entrance fee with the proceeds from the sale of their home. If you and your spouse are moving to a CCRC, expect to pay and entry fee between $200,000 and $300,000, plus a monthly charge around $2,000 per resident.[12]

The majority of CCRCs are run by non-profits, and many have a religious affiliation.

TIMELINE

Do not move into a facility unless you understand all the costs involved and how they fit within your budget. If your budget is on the lower side, you will want to start planning sooner because great places at budget prices fill up faster in most markets.

Look for a place that has a good value-to-cost ratio. You may not get everything on your wish list, so be willing to compromise on the items that are not as important to you.

If you have long-term care insurance and a significant nest egg saved up, pick your dream location. Enjoy your senior housing experience!

At some facilities, you can negotiate rates, take advantage of move-in specials, and add services at a discount. During your working career, you wanted to be paid for your work—so do senior living facilities.

There are many considerations more important than price. Do you want to be in a facility that serves low-quality food and whose residents and staff have low energy levels to save $500 a month? Most likely, you do not.

PLANNING

Why is it important to have your plan in place early? Without a good plan, you can run out of money. You do not want to outlive your money. If you have not been a master planner up to this point, now is your chance.

Have you found your perfect facility and created the budget to support it? If so, great job! Do not wait until your life starts winding down. Having your plan in place will give you the comfort and enjoyment to allow you to relax and have as much fun as possible.

PAYING FOR SENIOR HOUSING

The remaining sections in this chapter will focus on ways to pay for senior housing. Please consult your financial advisor, attorney, and advisory team to fill in all the details.

MEDICARE

Medicare is the primary health insurance for a large percentage of seniors in the United States. Medicare pays for medical costs but does not cover the cost of staying in a long-term facility, personal care, grooming, eating, transportation, bathing, and other personal care items that are considered non-medical.

Medical care at skilled nursing homes and some types of medical care at assisted living facilities (or at home), if administered by an independent third party, are covered by Medicare. If you qualify, Medicare will pay for a 20-day-or-less stay in a skilled nursing facility. After 20 days, you have to pay a portion of the costs until the 100th day. After 100 days, you are required to pay the full bill.[13]

MEDICARE SUPPLEMENTAL INSURANCE

Have you seen TV ads or received a flyer in the mail for Medicare supplemental insurance? Medicare supplemental insurance does not cover long-term nursing home care indefinitely but will help fill the gaps from Day 20 to Day 100 in a skilled nursing home facility. At the time of writing, Medicare will not pay for any care that lasts over 100 days.[14]

MEDICAID

If you have used all your out-of-pocket resources and are out of money, you can attempt to qualify for a state-run Medicaid program. Medicaid is for low-income individuals with minimal financial assets. If you are eligible, Medicaid will pay for nursing care (medical and non-medical expenses) and some home care expenses.

There are very few assisted living locations available for people on Medicaid. If you only need assisted living care and have very limited financial means, you will probably not find a place. In most states, you must spend your money until your assets total less than $2,000 before Medicaid will kick in.[15]

REVERSE MORTGAGE

A reverse mortgage is something you want to discuss with a financial advisor. It can be complicated and sometimes sounds too good to be true. Instead of taking out a mortgage and making payments to buy a house, a reverse mortgage company will put a lien on a home with high equity or is paid-off, and then make monthly payments to you.

A reverse mortgage is a way for you to take equity out of your house without selling it. The advantage of a reverse mortgage is you can stay in the home until you pass away or move (as long as you continue to pay taxes, insurance, and maintenance). Your estate will be reduced as you use the money you receive from the reverse mortgage to pay your living expenses.[16]

For some people, this may be the right choice; however, as with any financial instrument, you need to read the fine print and consult your team.

Beware: many people believe they cannot be foreclosed on and that the reverse mortgage company pays the insurance and annual property taxes for them.

The fine print of some contracts may state that not maintaining the home is considered a default against your reverse mortgage, and the lender can foreclose.

On some reverse mortgage agreements, if one of the homeowners dies, the spouse must pay back a large amount or the full amount of the loan. That is not the letter you want to get in the mail right after your spouse dies. Also, interest rates can be pretty high.[17]

THINGS TO WATCH OUT FOR

- Prices increasing for senior housing

- Annual rate increases

- Fine print

- Understanding the base price and any additional costs

- What Medicare will and will not pay for

- The qualifications for Medicaid

CHAPTER GOAL

The goal of this chapter is to provide information on senior housing costs and identify different methods to pay for it. Senior housing can be a big expense. If you do not have long-term care insurance, you can pay for care out of pocket, and when you run out of money, you can apply for Medicaid services.

When you finish this book, do not put it down and stop there. Start building out your plan. If you or someone on your team are nervous about where to start, contact us, and we will help you figure out the next step.

> TO FIND A **RAL** HOME NEAR YOU VISIT
> HTTPS://RALNA.ORG/FIND-A-HOME/

4
LONG-TERM CARE INSURANCE

According to a recent AARP study, one in four people currently over the age of 65 will incur more than $50,000 in lifetime out-of-pocket long-term care expenditures. Regular health insurance does not cover long-term care.

Many Americans believe that government funding will cover their long-term care needs as they age, but this is not the case for the majority of the population. Long-term care needs are generally paid out-of-pocket or through a Long-Term Care (LTC) insurance policy.

If you or your senior is younger than 60, it might be time to start looking at a long-term care policy. Policies are available for clients over 60, but the prices increase rapidly. If you need assistance bathing, walking, and performing daily errands, or are battling certain chronic health conditions, it will be difficult to get approved for a policy. So, the sooner you start planning, the better.

Depending on the policy, long-term care insurance starts to pay out when a senior cannot perform two of the six activities of daily living (ADL's):

- Eating
- Going to the bathroom
- Getting out of a bed or chair
- Walking
- Dressing
- Bathing

Long-term care insurance can cover assisted living, nursing care, Alzheimer's facilities, home modification, home care, adult day care, hospice care, and other expenses. Rates will vary based on your health and age, so consult your financial advisor for more details. Premiums for LTC insurance policies average $2,700 a year, according to the industry research firm Life Plans.[18]

LTC POLICIES AND COVERAGE

LTC insurance policies vary greatly, so referencing specific dollar amount limits and total values would not be helpful. Instead, we will use this section to help you navigate the types of policies in the market and the steps you can take to receive benefits from an existing policy.

The typical major components of a long-term care policy:

1. Daily benefit amount for different types of care
2. Waiting period (in days) before insurance kicks in
3. Maximum lifetime amount the policy will pay.

An alternative to LTC insurance is whole life insurance that you can draw from for long-term care. These hybrid policies will return money to your heirs if you never need long-term care and may be advertised as a long-term care rider with a permanent life insurance plan. This type of plan allows you to use the death benefit to cover long-term care needs. This may be packaged as a long-term care annuity.

When shopping for a new LTC policy, compare prices between different insurers as prices vary widely. If you are on a limited budget, remember *some coverage* is better than *no coverage*. Costs for policies will increase or decrease depending on the waiting period, daily limits, lifetime benefits, and cost of living adjustments.

Policyholders pay regularly scheduled premiums until they pass away or need to obtain care. The insurance company will pay out a daily or monthly benefit amount to pay for eligible long-term care services, such as hiring a home health aide, utilizing a daycare service, or entering an assisted living home.

Having a policy and knowing how to use it can yield many benefits. Although policies and conditions vary widely, our goal for the rest of this section is to give you a deeper level of knowledge to understand your long-term care policy better. We will elaborate on the common shared principles and components of most policies and connect you to additional resources you may need.

Like the other areas of this book, the information in this section is not meant to replace legal, tax, or financial advice.

LTC POLICY TERMS AND DEFINITIONS

An LTC insurance policy is an assigned contract between the insurance provider and the policyholder. Because policies, and the provisions in them, are unique to the policyholder, it is likely no two are the same (even if they are from the same insurance provider). Policyholders should review their policy to understand the covered benefits and provisions.

TYPE OF CARE

The policyholder must have a disability outlined in the policy to be considered "benefit eligible" before benefits are paid out from an LTC insurance policy. If the policyholder needs help with two out of six ADL's or needs supervision because of a cognitive impairment, most policies start paying out benefits after the elimination period has been fulfilled.

Most policies consider ADL assistance to be at least stand-by help to ensure someone stays safe. A few policies require the assistance to be fully hands-on before becoming benefit eligible. Some insurers accept the insured doctor's statement that care is medically necessary, while others my review the claim and make their own decision as to whether the care is medically necessary.

Custodial care such as helping with medicine, preparing meals, housekeeping, and other activities will not trigger benefits for LTC policies, but is a covered service by most plans once approved care begins.

POLICY REVIEW AND BENEFIT ELIGIBILITY

Locate your entire policy or request a copy from the insurance provider. If you are unsure if a policy exists, check for insurance statements where paperwork is kept and review bank account records for monthly deductions you do not recognize. Once you locate the policy, it is time to figure out what is covered and not covered. If you have a policy from an insurer that is no longer in business, a third-party administrator should be available to fulfill the benefits. Below are a few of the significant policy terms to understand.

ELIMINATION PERIOD

Under most policies, you are required to pay for long-term care services out of pocket for a predetermined amount of time (30 ,60, 90+ days) before the insurer starts reimbursing you for any care. The elimination period begins once the client is determined to be eligible for benefits and receive covered care as outlined in a written plan of care (receiving long-term care insurance benefits).

Typically, an elimination period is based on the days the policyholder receives services, not the number of calendar days since the first service. For example, let's say you receive covered services three times per week and have a 90-day elimination period. The elimination period would be fulfilled after 30 weeks because it is based on service days. If you receive care seven days per week, the days of service and the number of calendar days will be equal, so the elimination period is the same for either method. Check your policy for details on your elimination period.

RENEWABILITY

All LTC policies are guaranteed renewable, which means they can't be canceled as long as you pay your billed premiums on time and you were truthful on your health application.

NONFORFEITURE BENEFIT

If you drop your coverage, many LTC insurers will offer a cash refund of premiums paid or a reduced benefit from the original plan.

WAIVER OF PREMIUM

If you start to use your LTC insurance benefits, most policies waive or forgive your premiums. Check the policy to see if there are any restrictions or exceptions. Don't assume that premium payments automatically stop as soon as you have an approved claim or start receiving benefits.

BENEFIT TRIGGERS

Policies written after 1997 require that an insured be certified as "chronically ill" by a licensed health care practitioner. To qualify, the insured must be unable to perform, without substantial assistance, at least two ADLs for at least 90 days due to a loss of functional capacity or separately has a severe cognitive impairment requiring substantial supervision. The 90-day ADL is not a waiting period but a qualification that separates short-term needs where recovery is expected from ongoing long-term care needs.

TAX QUALIFIED

Policies written before 1997 were grandfathered in and are now considered tax qualified. Policies after 1997 must state on the coverage page if it is a tax-qualified policy or not. If the policy is tax-qualified, the benefits from the policy are usually received income tax free and monthly premiums may be deducted as a medical expense.

BENEFITS LIMITS

Most policies pay a daily maximum for care until you reach the lifetime maximum.

INFLATION PROTECTION

Cost of living increases to the daily benefits can be calculated as a simple increase or a compound increase. A simple increase adds a set dollar amount to the daily benefit each year. A compound increase will increase the daily benefit by a percentage of the current benefit.

SHARED BENEFITS

Some policies provide a benefit that can be drawn upon by either spouse if both spouses hold equal policies. If spouses buy policies at the same time, they have the option to share the total amount of coverage from both plans. If one spouse reaches the limit of their benefits, they can draw on their spouse's pool of benefits.[19]

WRITTEN PLAN OF CARE

The written Plan of Care is a document that describes the client's possible future chronic impairments and care needs and outlines how these needs will be met and who will provide the services. All claim requests require an accompanying written plan of care.

NEXT STEPS

Once you have determined the type of care you need and reviewed your policy, call your LTC insurance provider to confirm the answers to the questions below.

QUESTIONS TO ASK YOUR LTC INSURANCE PROVIDER

- Does the policy require an assessment, physician referral, prior hospital stay, or other prerequisites for benefits to kick in?

- How is Alzheimer's disease or dementia covered?

- What services are covered?

- What common services are not covered?

- How much does the policy pay per day, week, or month for each type of service?

- What is the maximum lifetime dollar amount the policy will pay?

- Does the policy have a maximum length of coverage period for each service?

- What are the elimination period terms?

- How many days must I wait before benefits begin for the different types of services?

- Do I pay for the services out of pocket during the elimination period?

- Is there a waiver of premium feature in my policy, and when does it start?

INFORMING YOUR CARE PROVIDER

Once you have selected a care provider for your long-term care needs (Chapter 2), give them the details of your LTC insurance policy. The care provider will need to supply documentation to help you initiate the claim. In some cases, the care provider may initiate the claim; other times, you or a family member may be responsible for initiating the claim. Communicate with your care provider to determine your elimination period so you can plan out care payments.[20]

SUBMITTING A CLAIM

When you need care and make a claim, the insurance company will review your medical documents. Before approving the claim, the insurer must approve your "plan of care."

BENEFIT PAYMENTS

Most policies pay benefits as expenses are incurred (benefits are only paid when the insured receives eligible services). The LTC insurance provider will review each claim to determine if it is for eligible services. Any benefits are paid to the policyholder or the provider. The coverage typically pays for either the expense or the dollar limit of the policy, whichever is less.

ASSIGNMENTS OF BENEFITS

Your LTC insurance policy is a contract between you and the insurance company. An Assignment of Benefit allows the insurance company to pay your care provider directly, which can make your life easier once you are settled into a facility and do not expect any changes of service. You should start the assignment of benefits process after the elimination period has ended and benefits are being paid out.

PREMIUM PAYMENTS

Continue making premium payments on your policy until you receive a fully-satisfied waiver of premium requirements. If the policy has a 90-day elimination period and a 90-day waiver of premiums, the policyholder would still need to make the premium payment for 180 days from the start of care or risk losing their benefits.

DENIED CLAIMS

What if your claim is denied? Claims are usually denied for one of two reasons. 1) The policyholder is not yet eligible for benefits or 2) the care provider selected by the policyholder is not covered by the insurer.

POLICYHOLDER NOT YET ELIGIBLE

If your claim is denied because the policyholder is not eligible, seek to clarify the impairment types and documentation needed to trigger benefits. Work with your healthcare provider to show in detail how the assistance or supervision needed meets the policy's benefit eligibility definitions.

CARE PROVIDER IS NOT COVERED

If the LTC insurance company does not view the provider as a qualifying provider, contact them directly or select a legal representative to work directly with the insurance company. Read the policy's provider definition carefully. If you are in a state that does not require licensing for certain care providers, this can cause a claim to be denied if the policy specifies care must come from a "licensed" provider. To resolve this issue, send your insurer more information about the provider or look for "exception" language in the policy.[21] Some policies only require a provider to be licensed if mandated by the state. If you want to use a provider that is not explicitly covered in the policy, most policies have a provision for an *Alternate Plan of Care*. The provision can allow you to use your selected provider as long as the insurance company is in agreeance.

APPEALS PROCESS

If your claim is denied, you may have the option to initiate an appeals process. Review your policy for specific appeal terms. You may be required to submit a written letter of appeal that explains why you are appealing the claim denial.

The appeals process may be challenging for seniors and the facilities. Often, the facility provider can help beyond what you can do or introduce you to an attorney or LTC claims specialist who are experts at navigating the LTC insurance claims process. Not only can they eliminate wasted hours making phone calls, they can also review the policyholder's records to determine if there was a past trigger event that should have allowed benefits to start.

SUMMARY

We hope after reading this section, you are more prepared and confident about your long-term care insurance benefits. If you have any questions about your policy or would like to connect with one of our LTC insurance referral partners, please contact us. We would love to help.

TO FIND A RAL HOME NEAR YOU VISIT

HTTPS://RALNA.ORG/FIND-A-HOME/

5

SOLUTIONS FOR YOUR CURRENT HOME

"I need to sell my house quickly! Can you come over to-day?" This was an urgent request to a real estate agent's office on a Tuesday morning. What could have happened to prompt someone who had lived in their house for over 40 years to call an agent they had never met and ask them to sell their home?

This client needed to sell her house quickly because she waited too long to ask for help. As the agent went over the homeowner's options, the owner became adamant about sell-ing that day: "I need to sell the home before I lose it. I have not been making the payments, and it is going to auction next week." The agent thought, "I wish she had called me six months ago for help. The outcome would have been much better."

The house was in rough shape, and the homeowner's kids and relatives were not helping. Fortunately, the agent sold the home before it went to auction, and the homeowner was able to keep some equity for retirement, and currently lives with family members.

NEEDS CHANGE

The house in which you raised your family and currently live may no longer fit your needs. There can be many reasons why a senior homeowner or their family may decide to sell their home. If your family is unsure what to do with the home, this chapter will guide you through the most common ways to sell a home and outline the pros and cons of each option.

CHANGE IN HEALTH

When someone no longer has the mobility or confidence to live at home, they usually sell the house and move. If that person does not have a support network in place or know someone who can move in with them, it is wiser to sell.

Changes in health can be sudden. One day you can be active, driving your car, and doing whatever you want, and the next you can be in the hospital recovering from emergency surgery—some events are difficult to predict.

We encourage you to plan and do as much as you can ahead of time. If disaster strikes, you and your family will be better prepared.

DEATH OF A LOVED ONE

For some, living in the house where their spouse passed away is an emotional burden. The pictures on the walls and memories are just too much to handle. In this situation, a change of location can sometimes help the healing process. Living in a house designed for a large family may be too much to handle.

DECIDING WHEN TO SELL

When you sell depends on the situation and recent events. Quick changes in your health and well-being may require faster decisions. If everyone involved is healthy and feeling great, and you are only evaluating what may happen down the road, you do not need to make these decisions quickly.

What options are available for your (or your parents') current house? It depends on how much time you want to invest, how soon you need to sell, how much money you have available for repairs and upgrades, and the condition of the house.

Whether you are in action or long-term preparation mode, do not wait until something happens to start planning. Dave Ramsey talks about financial planning and saving for things we know will happen in the future.

If and when your family faces a health challenge, dealing with it alone is going to be difficult. By putting your plan in place, you can focus entirely on the health challenge and not have to worry as much about your housing options—that part of the plan will already be in place, ready to be implemented.

BENEFITS OF A HAVING PLAN

Do you know how you will sell your home, who you will sell your home to, and when the plan will start? Are all your family members included in the plan, and is everyone in agreement about what will happen at each point in the journey?

Remember that you do not have to have everything perfectly planned out; there is no such thing as a perfect plan, but that should never be an excuse to not plan at all.

The benefits of creating your plan early are significant. If you plan the sale of your home ahead of time, you can usually get more money for your house, which means more choices for a senior housing location.

The best senior housing facilities may have waiting lists, and you have to move quickly when there is an opening. You do not want to find out that your name is next on the waiting list and only have a few weeks to plan the sale of your home.

If you have already spoken with housing professionals, you will be in a great position for a smooth transition. The goal is less stress and better outcomes. The results can be less favorable if you do not plan.

For instance, homes in many states usually sell faster and at a premium in the spring and summer months. Selling during the peak season makes sense to get as much as possible for your home.

If you know that your house needs some work and you want to update it to maximize your sale price, plan ahead to save money and reduce stress. Before you spend any money on your home, call a housing professional and get an expert opinion. Avoid unnecessary repairs or making upgrades that aren't consistent with other homes your area.

Things to Consider When Selling Your Home

Desired Outcome

What are your goals for when you sell your home?

You and your family need to map out what the desired outcome is for the sale of your home. Most goals involve a timeline, the closing or move out process, and the desired price range you will accept for the sale of your home.

Consult with a real estate professional that shares your core values and is someone you know, like, and trust. In addition, make sure that you are working with someone that has real expertise in the area you need help with.

Selling your home and transitioning to a new destination is a major life event. Make sure that you have the right team that can help you with all aspects of this move.

Finances

Houses cost money, even after they are paid in full. All homes have maintenance, tax, and insurance costs.

If your house is negatively affecting your finances, this could be a reason to sell it. Property taxes can be a serious problem for seniors who have purchased a home in an area where home prices have greatly increased in value. Many of our clients in such areas are on a fixed budget and cannot manage a large increase in their property tax bills—this is an area where seniors can get into trouble.

MOBILITY

If your mobility is severely restricted, your current home may not be the right fit, which could have a physical, emotional, or mental impact. We work with seniors who have not been upstairs in months or even years due to mobility issues.

EMOTIONAL TIES

Emotions are powerful forces subconsciously driving our decisions. The reasons you love your home may not be the same reasons that someone else does. Your emotions, memories, and attachments to the different parts of your home may be the opposite of what the potential buyer is feeling.

CONDITION OF THE HOUSE

Another step to successfully selling your home is getting an expert opinion on the condition of your home. Depending on where you live, some homes may sell well in any condition, while others really need to be fixed up to current standards.

When was the last time you remodeled your home? How does the condition of your home compare to the others for sale in your area?

Real estate is very localized, meaning that there can be a big difference in home prices and buyer demand in different states, cities, or neighborhoods. Even in your own neighborhood, it can be very different just one street over. So, when you are working with a real estate professional, make sure that they are an expert in your neighborhood. Choosing the wrong professional or trying to "go it alone" could cost you thousands of dollars, weeks of wasted time, and more stress and heartache.

Remember that when you are trying to sell, it is not about how you evaluate the home's condition; instead, the sale is based on the perception of buyers in your neighborhood and your local market. Therefore, it is important to look at the condition of your home through the lens of the buyers and how they will perceive it.

If your house needs a lot of updating, you may receive offers that you interpret as low. Sometimes it is challenging to know if someone making a "low" offer was trying to take advantage of your lack of real estate knowledge or if the "low" offer was really fair.

THE REAL ESTATE MARKET

As mentioned in the previous section, real estate is very localized, meaning that there are big differences between states, cities, neighborhoods, and even streets.

If you have lived in your house for a long time, you may not be familiar with your local real estate market. To simplify, we will cover the most important things you need to know.

MARKET CYCLES

The real estate market is like the elevator business—very up and down. Sometimes, it is *easy* to sell your home for a great price, and sometimes it is very *difficult* to sell your home.

Partnering with a real estate professional who can help you understand the current market in your local neighborhood will really help to give you an idea of what to do.

Different strategies work at different points in the real estate cycle, and knowing these strategies gives you an invaluable advantage when making your plan.

SELLER'S MARKET

In a seller's market, homes are in short supply, and there are lots of buyers that want to be in your neighborhood —it is easier to find a buyer. You can get a higher price and usually do not need to do as much updating to the home.

BUYER'S MARKET

In a buyer's market, there are many homes for sale, and buyers are in short supply. Between 2008 and 2011, numerous homes were up for sale and no one was buying them in the US.

Homes that are fully fixed-up for a great price normally go first in a buyer's market. In a seller's market, buyers will overlook cosmetic updates that are needed since they really want to get into a certain neighborhood and do not have many choices.

In a buyer's market, there are so many houses to choose from, and buyers normally pick the houses that are already updated instead of those that need a lot of work. Since there are many housing choices, buyers are not limited to purchasing homes that may need a lot of work.

Knowing what your strategy would be if you need to sell during one of these times is important for your outcome.

PHYSICAL ITEMS

If someone needs to move quickly, what is going to happen to all the physical items in the home? If your senior gets sick, who is going to sift through all the items in the home? How long will it take?

Believe it or not, not all senior citizens are minimalists. Years and decades of memories and special belongings can slowly collect over time, creating a vast inventory of physical items to go through, regardless of whether the move is imminent or in the future. After spending weeks or even months going through the items in their parents' home, my clients still feel like they are only scratching the surface.

TRASH OR TREASURE

An elderly lady had gone into a nursing home, and her adult son called a real estate agent to take a look at the house. For two months prior to this, her son had been spending nights and weekends cleaning the house.

When the agent walked into the home, he could not see the walls since objects and belongings were stacked all the way to the ceiling, with pathways forged through the items so as to walk to different parts of the house.

The agent turned to the seller's son and inquired, "Jeff, how are you progressing?"

Jeff replied, "Slowly."

His mom never threw anything away, and now her adult children had to go through it all.

If your parents have been storing things up, what would happen to all of those items if your parent were to suddenly pass away or needed to sell their home quickly?

As you create your plan, start thinking about reducing your possessions now. The more streamlined your home becomes, the more you can easily see and enjoy the items you really love (currently hidden by things you just like or tolerate). You will have less to worry about in the future when you move.

Often, our residents will take only 10% or 20% of what they had accumulated—or only those things they consider special—to their new house, leaving the rest for their housing professional to donate or discard. Some housing professional do not charge extra for this service—it is an added value that they extend to their sellers. If you are thinking about going down the investor route to dispose of your home this might be an option to save you some time and energy.

However, if you plan to sell your house to someone who will reside in the home, leaving your physical items behind will not be an option. Unless they are buying your furniture with the house, the home will need to be empty.

MISTAKES TO AVOID

Too many of our potential clients waste time, energy, and money because they do not fully understand how to deal with a home that is no longer serving its purpose. These are the biggest mistakes made by adult family members who are in charge of selling the property.

MISTAKE #1:
PICKING THE WRONG PERSON TO TAKE ADVICE FROM OR NOT TAKING ADVICE FROM ANYONE

There are some great real estate professionals in all markets but finding them requires work. In some states, it takes 10 to 20 times more training hours to receive a cosmetology license than a real estate license

Someone can cut your hair, make a mistake, and your hair will grow back. That person may be required to take 1000% to

2000% more training houses as someone who could be advising you on one of the largest financial transactions you may ever be involved in (i.e., selling your home).

On the investor side, it can be even worse. There are few or no state licensing requirements for an investor to buy your home. You could be working with a very reputable company or be approached by someone who has attended a three-hour weekend class and only knows the basics.

How will you know who to work with? The rest of this chapter and book will provide you with some strategies to help you make the right choices.

MISTAKE #2:
WORKING NIGHTS AND WEEKENDS ON FIXING UP A HOME TO INCREASE THE PURCHASE PRICE

This is a default decision for a lot of well-meaning children who think that if they fix up the house, it will sell for a lot more. Although a fixed-up home can sell for more, the type of repairs and updates you make require an in-depth knowledge of the local area.

Updating the home with materials that are more expensive than the area requires (over-rehabbing) is a waste of money. If you use materials that are below the neighborhood standard, buyers will not like it, and you will either not get much for the work or it will have to be redone to satisfy potential buyers.

Even if you predict the rehab requirements and repairs 100% correctly, who is going to do the work? If you are doing the work, how long will it take you compared to a professional, and how much is your time worth? If you have a full-time job and are trying to help your sick parent, you may not have as much time as you think.

Some of our clients find out after months of work that their efforts have not yielded the results they had expected. Before starting work on a house, consult a trusted advisor.

WAYS TO SELL YOUR HOUSE

There is no one-size-fits-all approach, so we are going to cover the three main ways you can sell a house and discuss the pros and cons of each.

Be cautious of anyone who tells you that their choice is the best in all situations. It depends on many factors, including your individual goals. We are not trying to persuade you to pick a particular strategy but are giving you the information to let you and your team decide what is best for you.

OPTION 1 — SELL THE HOUSE WITH AN AGENT

This is how most people sell their fixed-up, fully updated homes. Below are some sample questions to use when you are interviewing an agent. Each question is accompanied by a short explanation of its importance.

How long have you been in business?

This is very important—there is no substitute for experience. Let us emphasize: There is no substitute for experience. There are some long-time agents who are not very good at what they do, and there are some unseasoned agents who are very good at what they do.

Experience allows someone to see things differently. Work with an agent who has experience in similar situations. If an agent has been in the business for ten years but has only helped a few clients in your situation, that might not be good enough.

Are you a full-time or part-time real estate agent?

Don't leave one of the most important financial decisions of your life—selling a home—to an agent who has only sold a couple of homes and works part time. Would you want a part-time medical doctor who also has a day job doing something unrelated working on your heart?

We recommend you find a full-time agent who will be available when you need them and will likely have more experience.

Which neighborhoods do you specialize in?

Real estate is very localized. What works in one neighborhood may not work in another. Find an agent that knows your zip code and neighborhood and understands what buyers in that area want.

Have they helped buy or sell a house in your neighborhood in the last 12 months? If so, what was the outcome?

Can I contact your references?

Get references from people your agent has worked with in the past. How they treated their previous clients is likely an indicator of how you will be treated. You do not want to work with an agent that is hard to reach when you need them.

THINGS TO AVOID WHEN SELLING WITH AN AGENT

PRICING THE HOUSE TOO HIGH

This can happen for a number of reasons. It is difficult to know exactly what the perfect price for a house will be.

Sometimes, a seller wants a certain price and the real estate agent does not challenge them, there is a change in the market, or everyone was overly optimistic.

Once you list your home on the multiple listing service (MLS), that price is on record. If you have to lower the price, your listing may appear weak and cause offers to come in lower than expected.

PICKY BUYERS

When you accept a buyer's purchase contract, the buyer has a certain number of days to have an inspection completed (normally three to seven days). The buyer then has the option to cancel the contract or keep everything in place.

After viewing the inspection report, the buyer may ask you to make a lot of repairs or substantially lower the price.

THE HOUSE DOES NOT APPRAISE

In a seller's market, the prices of homes can be higher than ever before. The bank or financial institution will order an independent appraisal of the property before a loan is approved.

Sometimes, the appraiser who places the value on the home will not value it as high as the purchase price amount. The buyer can still buy your home but will need to make up the difference with their own money.

One of our referral partners was selling a home that was under contract for $210,000. Seven days before they were scheduled to close, the home was appraised for only $200,000. The company was in a quandary—they could not close unless the buyer came up with $10,000 in cash. In some markets, the buyers have the money, but they don't always want to use it. In the end, the seller had to lower the price, and the buyer put in some cash to make it happen. The closing stayed on schedule, but there were some bumps along the way.

Final Thoughts on Using a Real Estate Agent

If you sell with an agent in some markets, you will need to make repairs or upgrades for the house to sell at top dollar. Consider working with the best agent available—not just the best agent you are related to—so you can recoup your investment.

Deciding whether to use a real estate agent can be determined by market conditions, your needs, the amount of money you have available to put into the house, and how quickly you need to sell your home.

Typical clients that use an agent want to get the absolute most for their home. They are willing to wait a little longer if needed for the house to sell, and their homes are usually updated. If required, these clients have the time and money to make repairs or updates as the buyer demands.

Hiring a Family Member to be Your Agent

Hiring a relative to sell your house can be good or bad. You need a real estate professional that knows what they are doing, and that understands the local market.

The most significant risk in hiring a family member to represent you is if things do not go the way you want, you may not be comfortable firing them, which would be to your detriment. Also, how would that affect other family members?

Some individuals do not like to disclose finances to other members of the family.

OPTION 2 — UPDATE YOUR HOME BEFORE YOU SELL

TV shows do a great job of fueling the popularity of this strategy. Beware! Rehabbing your home is not as easy as they make it seem on tv house flipping shows. If your senior needs to move quickly, this strategy is no less enticing but much harder to execute.

Professionals who rehab several homes each year follow a detailed process with many steps. Homeowners who attempt to fix and flip their homes on their own are usually not satisfied with the results. What sounds like a good idea at the time rarely leads to the desired outcome.

Sometimes homeowners get halfway through making updates, become frustrated, and sell their homes to a local professional "as-is." If projects have not been carried out correctly or are unfinished, it can be more difficult to sell the house than if nothing had been done.

EVELIN NEEDS GOOD ADVICE

Evelin is a senior homeowner who wants to get as much as she can for her home. She confided with a real estate professional, "The equity of this home is all the money I have for retirement. I am 82 years old, and I have some money to put into the house if it will help sell it for more."

Two real estate agents told Evelin that she could sell the home "as-is" for $150,000. However, another agent (a full-time agent on our referral list) listened closely to Evelin's needs.

The third agent suggested another option—invest $15,000 to update the home, repair the foundation, fix a few cosmetic issues, and sell the house for more. Evelin rehabbed the home with her own money, using a local remodeling company.

After investing $15,000, she sold her home for $185,000.

$185,000 - $15,000 = $170,000.

Evelin made $20,000 more selling her home with this strategy. The closing process did take about two months longer, and she did have to deal with some stress. She could no longer live in the house, and she had to pay $15,000 upfront for the repairs.

You won't get something for nothing, but it was worth it to Evelin in this case. It was possible that the housing market could have started to slow down or prices could have dropped quickly while the house was being repaired, impacting her profitability. However, Evelin was willing to take these risks.

When Things Don't Go as Planned

Sally was 78 years old and lived by herself. She had experienced a fall and no longer felt safe living alone. Beth, Sally's oldest daughter, called a local real estate office for advice. Sally fell again and was now in a physical therapy facility. Beth did not expect her mom to be able to move back into her house.

The plan was to move Sally into an assisted care facility. Beth was asking about what they should do with Sally's home. She told the real estate agent that they were considering updating the house with new floors, windows, and paint inside and outside of the house so they could sell it for more money. If you are a contractor with lots of extra time and money for materials, this may be a great option. Beth and her husband both had full-time jobs, and they lived about 20 miles from the house.

The real estate agent asked Beth how much time she needed each week to take care of her family (she still had teenage kids at home) and check on her mom. Beth had a limited capacity for handling all these demands. Rehabbing a home during a medical crisis of a family member presents significant challenges.

UNDERSTANDING A HOME'S VALUE

Remember that every neighborhood is unique. The right flooring or finishes in your neighborhood may be a waste of time and money in a different neighborhood.

Certain repairs increase the value of your home more than others. For example, if you replace the air conditioning unit, you will normally get a small premium above what you paid. Homebuyers like to buy houses that have a new A/C unit, but it is not going to yield the seller a lot when compared to the cost.

Installing a $5,000 air conditioner will not increase the value of a home by $15,000; it's more likely to add $5,000 or $6,000 and usually helps the home to sell faster. You will probably recoup your $5,000 investment but won't make much more over that amount.

THE SPEED OF THE REPAIR WORK

If you are doing updates to the home yourself, you probably do not have as much time to devote to it as a full-time contractor does. Also, you likely work a lot slower than a professional contractor. While it might take a three-man crew (charging $400) one day to install new flooring, it may take you three to seven days, or even an entire month.

Do you want to invest your time and energy in fixing up a home or spend time with your loved ones? Your return on time invested is not going to be very high, unless you are an expert.

Consider spending time with your aging relative instead of rehabbing their home. If your loved one has just moved into an assisted living or senior facility, remember that the average stay in an assisted living center in the United States is around 28 months.[22]

OPTION 3 – SELL TO AN INVESTOR

A good real estate investment company will share your core values and provide you with a real service. Make sure to work with a company that has high standards. Like real estate agents and contractors, real estate investors seek to make a profit from their work. Real estate investors take the most risk.

A real estate agent can tell you that your house will sell for any amount you want to hear. When the house does not sell for that amount, they can drop the price. A contractor works on your house but does not assume the risk of selling it. A real estate investor buys your house and takes all the rehab and selling risks.

Normally, you get the least amount for your home when you sell to an investor. The investor does not plan live in the home, so the home is not worth as much to them as to someone who will. Also, the investor plans to spend months and potentially tens of thousands of dollars improving the home.

One of our referral partners recently bought a fixed-up home from a client. Since the house was fixed up, they told the client that they would net more money selling their home with a real estate agent or directly to a buyer who was going to live in it. It would take longer, they would have to open their home to showings, and possibly deal with any repairs required after the inspection process.

Although the all-cash offer was $10,000 less than the best estimate of selling through an agent, the client chose the cash offer instead. She and her husband were moving to a 55+ independent living community and did not want the hassle of selling her home during the upcoming winter. The homeowner told the investor, "I can get more money; I cannot get any more time."

Selling to an investor does have benefits. Clients who are a good fit for this want or need to sell their homes quickly usually can close within 30 days or less of going under contract.

Ideal clients for this option do not have much money to make repairs or updates or those whose houses are in rough shape with a fair amount of deferred maintenance.

QUESTIONS FOR REAL ESTATE INVESTORS

How do you determine a fair price for the home?

The biggest problem with the term "fair price" is a *fair for whom*? A "fair price" normally represents a range. A client wants to get as much as they can for their house, and a business wants to make as much as it can for its bottom line.

It seems like the client and investor are on opposing sides. There is a way to engage in this price topic so that the client and company are on the same side.

The price has to be a win-win for both parties. The homeowner needs to get a fair price they are happy with that reflects the current condition of the home and the amount of time, energy, and money needed to get the home to market standards. The person who does that work (the investor) needs to make a fair profit for that type of risk.

The fastest way to get the price you want for your home is to tell the interested party what you want for the home or what you think is a fair price. Be open to information about the true fair market value of your home.

Sometimes, clients will not say what they really want for their house, worrying that it will be lower than what the investor will offer. Nine times out of ten, however, the number the client wants is higher than the true value. Communicating this to your investor is a great way not to waste time and move on to finding the right solution for you.

While price is important, there are other things to consider such as time and energy? How much is your time worth? The most important thing to consider (other than price) is who you are working with. If an investor says they are going to buy your house for a great-sounding number, but they don't show up at the closing, what did that great number really mean? Nothing!

It's important to understand why the investor needs to make a profit. Working on a house as an investor carries a great deal of risk. For example, house prices could go down by the time the investor sells the home.

There are factors you cannot see that affect the value of your home. Are there termites in the walls or under the pier and beam foundations? Is there an undiscovered plumbing issue that could cost $10,000 to fix? Is there mold in the bathroom that requires special services to treat? If an old home is being sold, there are things no one knows about until repairs start. Do you want to take that risk on, or do you want to transfer that risk to an investor?

How will you pay for the house?

Not everyone who says, "I pay cash for houses" is actually going to buy your home. Instead, they may wholesale your house to another buyer.

A wholesaler is an investor that puts your home under contract for an agreed-upon price and sells the contract to a cash buyer at a higher price.

WHOLESALING EXAMPLE

You call the number on a sign that says, "Jesse buys houses," and Jesse comes over to view the home and agrees to buy it for $100,000. He may or may not tell you that he has no plans to buy your home with cash or that he does not have the ability to do so.

Jesse tells you that some of his "partners" or "contractors" need to look at the house before the closing. Jesse is showing the house to actual cash buyers come who will buy the house for $110,000.

A cash buyer who likes the house agrees to buy it from Jesse for $110,000, and Jesse "assigns" the contract to the cash buyer. At closing, if all goes according to plan, the cash buyer pays $110,000 for the house, the client receives $100,000, and the wholesaler—Jesse—receives $10,000.

If you had worked directly with the cash buyer directly, would you have received $10,000 more?

Wholesaling has come under fire in some states because when done improperly, it can be misleading to sellers.

If Jesse came to your home and told you, "I am not going to buy the house, but I will market this house to my large list of cash buyers. One of them is going to buy your house, and I am going to make a profit off of that," then that is fine as long as you get the price you want for your house and you know what is going on. If Jesse is adding value for you, there is nothing wrong with him getting paid.

You should beware of inexperienced wholesalers. Many new investors start by wholesaling houses. These investors could put your home under contract (control) and be unable to find a buyer.

Some companies buy and later sell properties without working on them, but they always purchase houses with their cash and sell them *after* the homeowner has been paid. New wholesalers may never buy your home after putting it under contract.

One of our referral partners offered to buy a home for $75,000 and was told by the client that another investor offered $85,000. That investor was a new wholesaler who did not know what he was doing. The new wholesaler filled out a contract to purchase the house but never planned to actually do so. Three days later, this wholesaler called our referral partners office asking if they wanted to buy the home.

Three weeks later, the wholesaler canceled the contract because he was unable to sell the house to another buyer. There were a couple of clauses in the contract that allowed him to cancel with no penalty.

The homeowner believed their house had been sold and had already started to move out. They planned to use the money from the closing to put down on a new house. The homeowner called our referral partner, and the home was sold in less than seven days.

Can you provide Proof of Funds?

A proof of funds letter is issued by a bank or financial institution and shows that a buyer has the means to pay for the house. Do not be afraid to request a proof of funds letter, even from investors. An investor can also show you a bank statement as financial proof.

If I make repairs to the house, can that increase the value, and by how much?

Most investors can get the work done on houses much cheaper than a homeowner can. When a client does the work on a house that they are going to sell to an investor, it is usually not worth the time, energy, or money.

In what condition can we leave the house if we sell to you?

Many sellers do not realize that most investors will not charge additional fees to leave items in a house. Ask the investor if their price includes leaving extra furniture, household items, or trash behind.

Usable items that have are left behind can be donated to local charities. If you are selling a house to an investor while other important events are happening, you want to be present and focused on those—do not clean out the entire house if you do not have to.

When can we close?

This is important to know if you are selling the home to buy another home or pay medical bills. Most investors can close on a home within 30 days depending on the condition of the title.

Investors generally pay all of the closing costs. The homeowner would be responsible for paying the taxes on the property and any liens or mortgages.

Do you have any references?

Read reviews online (Home Advisor, Angie's List, and The Good Contractor's List), look the business or person up on social media (Facebook and LinkedIn), or check with the Better Business Bureau. These are good starting points, but don't always tell the whole story.

As long as a business owner pays monthly fees to be a member of the Better Business Bureau and responds to any complaints, the owner will maintain an "A" rating. Speak directly to previous clients over a phone call to gauge if someone is the right company for you to partner with.

What does the closing process look like?

Closing processes vary from one state to the next. Never perform a closing anywhere except in an attorney's office or at a title company. Read the fine print so you know exactly what closing costs you are paying. Sometimes, an investor only pays half of the closing costs.

Who pays additional lawyer's or closing costs?

Probate or other legal issues can result in additional closing costs. Know who will be responsible for paying these. If someone with a power of attorney is involved, make sure that all relevant documents are presented to the title company or attorney. The title company will review the documents, confirm the documents are valid, and verify that the person has the power to sell the home. If the documents are not valid, closing could be delayed.

What to Avoid When Selling to an Investor

Foreclosure Deadline

Investors can help homeowners in different stages of the foreclosure process. When you do not repay a loan on time, the mortgagee has the right to force the sale of your home. Unfortunately, when seniors sometimes get into this situation, they get nervous, and are afraid to tell family members what is going on financially, so the situation just gets worse. Homeowners will reach out to sell their homes only two or three days before the foreclosure auction. Sometimes, the real estate professional can help, but this is not always possible.

We recommend that you talk to your team of advisors (accountant and attorney) and call your lender to try to work something out. Do this as soon as you think you may miss a payment. If you are in a tough situation, most mortgage companies will work with you. If too much time has passed before you pay, or if you do not contact them, the creditor will not be as flexible.

Chapter Goal

Our goal for this chapter has been to help you better understand all the factors that help you decide whether to sell your home and different methods to sell your home. Planning ahead is the key.

6
AGING IN PLACE

HOME ALONE

Recently, a client (Mark) called one of our partner offices and told them that his mom, Betty, was living alone. Mark felt Betty should sell her home and move to an assisted living facility, and he wanted some advice on their options.

Betty lived alone, and she needed some extra help with the house. It was literally falling apart. Mark had a pretty demanding job, and he lived about 30 miles away, so it was difficult to always be there when his mom needed help.

The real estate agent suggested all the stakeholders (Betty and her three adult children) meet at the house so they could review all the options. When everyone arrived, they gathered around the kitchen table. Mark told Betty he was concerned for her safety. Betty retorted, "Well, there is no way I am ever leaving this house!"

This story plays out every day in our market and all over the United States. Betty wanted to keep her home, so the agent's job was to help them come up with a solution so she could safely stay in her home, and her children wouldn't have to worry.

It is hard to make everyone happy. Betty was still of sound mind, so even if the choice was unpopular with her family, it was hers to make.

In this chapter, we discuss how to build out a roadmap to allow a senior to stay in their home as long as they want.

Seniors who want to keep their home either want to:

- Stay in the home, even if their health is failing; or

- Keep the home in the family (allow another relative to live in it or pass it down to a son or daughter).

These are separate (sometimes closely connected) issues, so we will spend time discussing each one. Staying in your home—even when your health is failing—and passing your home down to your family members are possible outcomes. The sooner you plan for these events, the better the result will be.

NON-NEGOTIABLES

Staying in your home has two major components:

1. Resident's needs, such as safety and security

2. Homeownership responsibilities, such as maintenance and financial obligations

If you can meet both of these needs, staying in the home can be a great option. Otherwise, staying in your home may not be the best choice.

Keeping a home in the family is possible, but different challenges exist. Whether the house is vacant, or someone is living in it, the taxes, mortgage, and insurance need to be paid and kept current. Maintenance schedules need to stay current to avoid HOA or local code enforcement violations and prevent the property value from decreasing.

Leaving a house vacant for an extended period can make it a target for break-ins or other crimes, such as vandalism. Also, maintenance schedules may be disrupted, leading to major problems with systems in the home.

Keeping your home is a lot more complicated than selling it. When you sell your home, you do not have to worry about it anymore after the closing—the pros and cons of owning that home are now someone else's concern.

The path you choose will be depend on your individual goals. The purpose of this chapter is to identify things to think about as you craft your plan.

QUESTIONS TO CONSIDER

- What recent event has you thinking about staying in your home?

- What recent event makes keeping your home a concern or a challenge?

- If your health condition changes, will you be able to stay in your home?

- What changes, if any, would you need to make to your home?

If a homeowner is experiencing limited mobility, home maintenance may be neglected, and conditions in the home can quickly deteriorate.

WHO WANTS TO BUY THE HOME?

If you are in the early stage of planning, ask your family members if anybody wants to buy or lease the house when the senior moves. If you don't ask, you won't know—never assume anything, and involve all stakeholders when you start your plan.

If the buyer is a family member, they must have the desire and capacity to buy the home. If a family member is really excited about buying the home but has neither the money nor sufficient credit, that is a capacity issue. You should probably not sell your house to anyone who does not have the capacity to buy any house on your street.

SUDDEN ILLNESS OR INJURY

Elaine fell while she was at home and had to be hospitalized. Her son hoped she would make a full recovery and then return home. For six months, he worked during the day, would spend time with his family and do things around the house before visiting his mom at the rehab center in the evenings, and took care of his mom's house on the weekends.

After six months, the family realized Elaine would not be fully independent again or able to return home. It was tough for her son to accept that things would no longer be the same. He had grown up in the home, and he loved it.

Although Elaine wanted to go back to her home when she got better, many questions still needed to be answered.

- When will mom be well enough to leave the facility?

- If mom gets healthy again, who will help at home?

- What things need to be done to the house now and in the future to keep it up?

BUILDING A ROADMAP TO KEEP YOUR HOME

- Do not wait until it is too late.

- Do not wait until somebody gets sick.

- Do not wait until somebody has to move into a nursing home to create a plan—do it now.

Use the checklists and questions in this chapter to start a discussion and put your plan in place.

THREE BENEFITS OF PLANNING EARLY

BENEFIT #1
MAINTAINING THE VALUE OF THE HOME

If the plan is to keep the home, preserve as much of the house's market value as possible. The plan right now may be to keep the house forever but plans sometimes change. If an increased level of care becomes necessary, that could be expensive, and the home may need to be sold to pay for it.

Keeping the home in a condition that will attract the highest market value will be very beneficial.

ACCESS TO FUTURE CAPITAL

If you need to borrow money in the future, it can be borrowed against the house's appraised value without selling it. The higher the value, the more funds will be available.

Homeownership is one of the biggest net worth components for many Americans, especially when the homeowner has paid off the mortgage. The next section includes tips to maintain the property's condition and value.

PROPERTY CONDITION

Many seniors let maintenance slide as their expenses increase and their income remains fixed.

For example, if a senior on a fixed budget is living alone and one bathroom needs repairs and is no longer usable, there are two choices: fix it and maintain the home's value or you could just leave it.

Similar isolated events can build up slowly over a 10- or 15-year period, and when the senior gets ready to sell their home or make repairs, those little projects have turned into seven or eight big projects.

This is called deferred maintenance. So, if the plan is to keep the home, make sure that you set a realistic budget for the monthly and annual maintenance. Set aside 1-3% of the total value of the home for maintenance every year. For a $200,000 house, expect to spend $2,000 - $6,000 per year on maintenance.

If the home is older, and you estimate maintenance costs will be 3%, set aside $400 per month so you have $4800 saved.

MAJOR SYSTEM COSTS

Every major component of the home has a certain lifespan. You have probably heard, "They do not make them like they used to." That is a true statement today.

Below are some rough estimates of how long your home's major systems will last and typical replacement costs. Many factors affect lifespan and cost—use these averages as the starting point for a budget. If you need access to a contractor for your home, feel free to reach out to us, and we will introduce you to someone in our trusted network.

ROOF REPLACEMENT

A new roof should last anywhere from 10 to 20+ years but it depends on where the house is located. For an 1,800 sq ft home, a new roof will typically cost from $6,000 to $12,000.

FOUNDATION REPAIR

Repairs to damaged foundations are expensive, and a weak foundation also affects other areas of the home, such as plumbing problems.

If you notice cracks on the outside of the house or large cracks on your interior walls, you may have a foundation issue.

Consider having a licensed structural engineer who is familiar with your area perform an inspection of the foundation. A structural engineer is not trying to sell foundation work; their job is to determine if there is active movement in a home and create a plan to fix it. Foundation repair can cost from $5,000 to over $15,000.

HEATING, VENTILATION, AND AIR CONDITIONING (HVAC)

Modern HVAC systems usually last between eight and 12 years. Older units seem to last longer, but every machine has an expiration date. Too often, these systems break down in the middle of the summer when it is sweltering outside.

Budget accordingly. Clients who regularly change their air filters (monthly) and have their units serviced each year have reported a much longer lifespan for their equipment.

The cost to replace HVAC equipment (inside and outside) ranges from $6,000 to over $10,000.

PLUMBING

Plumbing problems and the costs to fix them can vary. If your house has ever flooded due to a sewer backup or a busted hot water heater, you know what we mean. Repairs like a leaky faucet can be minor, or extensive, like sewer pipe replacement.

One of our senior friends received an unusually large water bill one month. She had a plumber test the water and sewer system—there was a slab leak at her home.

The pipes under the house had a crack and were leaking water, causing the soil to swell up and the foundation to buckle, which damaged the walls. As a result, some doors in the house could not open while others could not close.

The plumber performed a leak isolation test and located the issue. The homeowner's insurance did not cover all of the costs, and she had to pay a few thousand dollars out of pocket. Plumbing repairs can range from $200 (basic repairs) to over $15,000 (major repairs).

ELECTRICAL

Your electrical system should be low maintenance. If the home's original electrical panel is out of code or has aluminum wiring, look into getting those items replaced and up to the current standards. At the very least, have your system inspected by a licensed electrician to ensure that you and your home are safe.

Any system can require minor repairs. If you add extra lights or outlets to your existing system, make sure that your electrical box can handle the increased load.

Electrical repair costs range from $150 (small repair) to $3,000 (to replace an electrical panel) and can exceed $10,000 (if you need to rewire the house and replace old aluminum wiring with copper wiring).

BENEFIT #2
GETTING THE RIGHT HELP YOU NEED

What are your first steps if you are in the fast-track planning mode? If there is an illness or sudden health crisis, addressing this situation right away is more important than the value of the house. You want to be able to live as comfortably and safely in your home as possible.

Start thinking about who might help in the short term. Also, determine what local resources and agencies are available to help in your home if needed.

Additional help can range from mobility aids like ramps instead of stairs, meal preparation, and transportation to doctor appointments. If you plan to stay in your home and need extra help, who can assist you with these needs?

BENEFIT #3
CREATING A SMOOTH TRANSITION

To ensure a smooth transition, address immediate concerns and then set up a plan for the future. Here are a few questions to help with this:

- If there is a health or mobility issue, who will be the caretaker or assistant?

- How will you find the right caretaker to help you in your home?

- Who will help with the home maintenance?

- How will this home be passed on (given or sold to a family member)?

- Who will take future ownership of the home, and when will it happen?

- Who will be in charge of this process?

- Did you document this process in collaboration with an attorney?

LEGAL MATTERS

You have probably read about celebrities, with access to finances and attorneys, who pass away with no will. Consult an attorney and get these documents together today. Some of our clients do not create a will, trust, or other planning documents because they think these are too expensive.

How much is it worth to you to have plans in place that can be followed during difficult times? These documents are an investment, not an expense. There are professionals who work with people on a budget; however, do not decide purely on price.

An attorney can create a trust so that your assets would not have to go through the probate process but would pass directly to your heirs.

A will goes through the county probate process and is contestable (challengeable) in court. A will and all the assets in it also become public record.

Make sure you work with a legal professional who specializes in this type of work. We have seen many families that had legal documents created only to find out later the documents were not valid.

WHAT IS THE PROBLEM COSTING YOU?

Keeping a home or not keeping a home is a very personal choice that depends on several factors. Paying someone to maintain an older home can be costly, especially if you are on a fixed budget.

Some homeowners decide to keep their homes based on their emotions and feelings, and others choose to keep their homes because they cannot afford a senior living facility.

When deciding, you should also consider the amount of time you will spend maintaining your home. Is it a comfortable and safe place to live? How much time are you going to be spending at your home? Golden years are supposed to be fun, and your residence should be an exciting part of your adventure, where you will feel safe and enjoy life.

Housing decisions will affect relationships. When you are contemplating selling or keeping your home, you may notice relatives you have not seen in years will try to give you advice. Figure out who is looking out for your best interests and only have those people on your team.

Expect the unexpected! Only share your plans with your inner circle.

THE PERFECT WORLD

In a perfect world:

- You have a plan in place.

- You have made the necessary modifications to the home, or you know who is going to make them.

- You have set up a maintenance team, yard crew, handyman, and tree-trimming person.

- Your legal team created necessary legal documents.

- You are in a great position.

- You can worry less and enjoy more.

MAINTAIN THE HOME

At this point, there is a budget for your annual maintenance and money has been set aside in a separate account to pay these expenses. A team of professionals has been identified to call when needed.

If the home is vacant and the goal is to pass it on to the next generation, the challenges are different. Perform regular maintenance as if someone were living there.

If possible, have a family member that you know, like, and trust, have live in the home to help maintain it, even if they only live there a few days per week.

RETROFIT THE HOME

Existing homes may need modifications such as handrails, ramps, and other mobility aids to be functional. Upfront costs for the changes may be expensive, but it can be a lot cheaper than moving to a hands-on facility. Also, staying in the home can be less burdensome than moving in with a family member.

Consult a specialist in senior home modifications, such as a *Certified Aging-In-Place Specialist* from The National Association of Home Builders. For more information, visit www.nahb.org.

These specialists understand the unique needs of seniors and can make the necessary home modifications.

Below are some tips on tackling projects such as creating a walk-in shower, adding handrails, or whatever you need to make life a little easier.

CONTRACTOR TIPS

- Interview only contractors that are insured and bonded, so you are protected if the contractor makes a mistake, breaks something, or is injured.

- Referrals from friends and family are a great way to find a reputable contractor. It helps to know someone who has had a great experience with them.

- You must check references for every contractor you hire. Let us repeat: Check their references—this is very important.

- Obtain at least three bids before selecting a contractor and starting work.

It is good to have options. Although the price is important, other factors such as reputation, quality, and speed to complete the job are also important considerations.

WHERE TO START

Determining which modifications to make first will depend on the senior's current needs. When a senior starts losing mobility, modifications to the bathroom, such as converting the bathtub to a walk-in shower, and adding handrails in the home are typically among the first changes that are made.

STEPS AND OTHER ELEVATIONS

Elevations likes steps and staircases can be hazardous for seniors with mobility challenges. Converting stairs into a ramp and adding handrails can help.

LIGHTING

Many accidents happen at night when seniors are moving around with no light or low lighting. Increase the lighting in your home by adding new light fixtures or using removable touch lighting and plug-in nightlights. Consider setting the lights on a timer to turn on automatically at night.

SECURITY

Senior citizens are often targets for criminals and thieves and adding a security system can keep the bad guys away. Outdoor lighting with motion sensors adds another layer to your home's security.

A wearable panic button is another deterrent that can also notify emergency personnel if the wearer falls. (You can also purchase standalone systems to request help if there is an accident in the home.)

SCOOTERS AND WALKERS

If a mobility aid is not necessary all of the time, they can really help when a break is needed. Some walkers have a built-in seat to allow the user to rest on long-distance treks.

Electric scooters can be used both outside and inside the home. Most are narrow enough to get around your home without causing damage. They can be heavy, so plan accordingly; lighter models are available.

Bringing in Help

Seniors at different stages in their lives could need two types of care if they remain in their home: skilled medical care and personal care.

Medical care involves a trained medical professional coming into the home to help with medical needs, such as providing medicine or therapy.

Personal care might include taking a senior to doctor's appointment, shopping, food preparation, bathing, and helping with eating, dressing, or laundry.

Many different agencies provide these types of care. Below are some questions you should ask when interviewing a home care agency:

- What services do you provide?

- How long have you been providing these services?

- Are you licensed by the state?

- How do you structure your fees?

- Do you perform background checks on your staff?

- How will you communicate with family members?

- Are your caregivers available 24 hours a day?

FINDING CAREGIVERS

Referrals from people you know, like, and trust are a great place to start. Local agencies can also be a great resource

Perform reference checks on providers or agencies before bringing anyone into the home and require a copy of their proof of insurance. Seniors can be trusting people, so ensure another member of the advisory team is present during an interview to ensure that there are no red flags.

ARE THEY COMING BACK?

What happens if your senior leaves their home due to a medical issue, and moving back is no longer an option? Do they want to keep the house or sell it? Remember, if you decide to sell the house, the better condition it is in, the more you will get for it.

If your senior needs minor medical attention or is admitted to the hospital, do not put the home on the market the next day. After three to six months, your team will have a good sense of what will happen with your loved one and what should be done with the house.

If the goal is to keep the house in the family and pass it on to a family member while the senior homeowner is still alive, double-check the laws in your state. Consult an attorney for the best route.

If your senior currently receives government aid for their living expenses, double-check the rules and requirements.

The government provides aid for seniors who experience financial hardship. A senior who owns a property that is paid in full does not have a financial hardship.

Family members often ask if they can transfer a home into someone else's name so it's not on their senior's balance sheet.

Consult an attorney before transferring real estate into someone else's name. Also, when planning to transfer property to a family member, consult an accountant to see if there are any tax implications. In some states, clients may use a quitclaim deed to pass real estate to a family member when there is no financial transaction involved.

THINGS THAT CAN GO WRONG

Your senior's physical condition can deteriorate rapidly. Sometimes, the senior does not want to let on that things are not going well for fear of losing their independence. Create an environment where the senior will tell the members of the team what is happening.

Trust but verify. If the house is vacant, keep it under close watch. Have all of your legal documents ready in case a relative becomes unruly.

SAMPLE PLAN

Jeff wants to live in his home for as long as possible. He has budgeted $300 per month for home maintenance. When he needs personal or medical care for more than eight hours a day, he wants to move to an assisted living facility where more advanced care is available.

Jeff's first preference is to live with a family member, as long as he is not a burden. If he is unable to live with a family member, he wants to move into the least restrictive senior facility possible.

If he is unable to move back into his house after living in a senior facility for six months, he wants his oldest daughter to sell his home and put the money into an account to pay his living expenses.

After he passes on, he wants his oldest daughter to execute the trust with a specific attorney and follow the guidelines therein.

How We Can Help?

An ounce of prevention is worth a pound of cure. If you reach out to us, we will refer someone to you to help with the maintenance for your house.

> **To find a RAL home near you visit**
> **HTTPS://RALNA.ORG/FIND-A-HOME/**

Chapter Goal

The goal of this chapter is to share what to consider when deciding whether keep a home and some things to look out for in the process.

FAMILY SUPPORT

Every day in America,10,000 people turn 65.[23] Who will care of them? Will their care be paid with government funds, personal savings, or by family members?

The family members of seniors face unique challenges. Will the last years of your senior family member's life be enjoyable for everyone or a great source of conflict?

FAMILY IMPACT

According to Rich Johnson at the Urban Institute, about 10% of Americans over age 65 have long-term care insurance.[24]

How will the other 90% of seniors pay for senior housing, and what impact will that have on their families?

If your relationship with your senior family member is strained or their condition quickly worsens, this transition can be more difficult. When you have to start caring for an aging family member, talk to all the family members and determine who will contribute financially or physically to the care.

Even if no one wants to help, it is better to know that from the start than to assume everyone will help. The best thing to do is to come up with a plan and work it out together.

If your senior needs more advanced help, who in your family is the best candidate to assist in this area? Or will you need to bring in outside help?

OTHER THINGS TO CONSIDER

Family members of seniors face many struggles, which are outlined below with some recommendations on how to handle them. The questions in this and previous chapters are not a replacement for consulting professional counselors, advisors, and attorneys. They are a great starting point for getting some concerns out in the open so you can come up with a plan to resolve them.

The questions, concerns, and challenges listed below have been sent in by family members of our senior clients. We hope these concerns and recommendations give your family clarity.

LACK OF APPRECIATION FROM SENIORS BEING TAKEN CARE OF BY FAMILY MEMBERS

Think back to when you were a kid and your parents spent hours preparing a gourmet meal. How did you show your appreciation? "No thanks, I want something else!"

Maybe you were the exception. If you are a parent, you may hear that all the time. It's hard not to take it personally when you are not appreciated.

Will you be appreciated all the time when you are taking care of a senior family member? It depends. Even if your senior has a great disposition, it can be challenging when they are sick or in pain

It is fine to tell your family member how you feel, but things may not change. Be patient and find another family member or a friend you can confide in.

STRAINED RELATIONSHIPS BEFORE CARE BEGAN

If your relationship with your senior was strained before they got sick or needed your help, it is probably not going to get any better when more emotional, financial, and physical stress gets piled on top.

Consider family counseling. The more you can include a trained third-party advisor to help you, the better. Counseling can come from a trained family member, a church leader, or a private counselor. Most strained relationships did not get that way overnight, so do not expect the tension to dissipate immediately. However, you can start making progress today.

CARING FOR SENIORS WITH MEMORY ISSUES

Your mood and energy will influence your senior. If you are positive and happy, it will encourage them and give you more patience. Speak to your senior in simple sentences and ask questions that require 'yes' or 'no' answers. If your senior does not reply right away, be patient.

If you need your senior to complete a task that involves many steps, start with step 1 and do not talk about step 2 until step 1 is complete. If your senior gets mad at you, talk about something else, go for a walk, or get something to eat. A change in scenery can help redirect the issue.

Sometimes, looking at old photos can be a fun activity. Many seniors with memory issues cannot remember what you told them to do 30 minutes ago, but they can remember what was going on in a photo 30 years ago.[25]

MAJOR HEALTH ISSUES

According to a recent survey by the AARP Public Policy Institute and National Alliance for Caregiving, one in three people caring for someone at home hired paid help to assist them.

If you are caring for a senior at home, start planning to get extra help, even if you do not need it right now. If your senior is over 55 years old and certified by the state as in need of nursing home-level care, find out if a PACE program (for people on Medicare or Medicaid) is offered in your area. These programs cover in-home care, doctor care, and transportation. For more details, visit *https://www.medicare.gov/your-medicare-costs/get-help-paying-costs/pace*.[26]

FINANCIAL ISSUES

The costs for senior care can be enormous. Hopefully, you got this book early in the process, and you can start working backward to create a plan.

Lack of communication about money contributes to the stress. Many families we work with do not talk about money until they have to.

Also, look into local programs for seniors offered by religious institutions and not-for-profit organizations, such as United Way.[27]

ONE SIBLING DOING ALL THE WORK OR PREVENTING OTHERS FROM SEEING THE SENIOR

The sooner you start mapping out the roles and expected contributions for everyone on the advisory team, the sooner you will get clarity on what the next steps are. If you are the sibling doing all the work required to take care of your senior, let other family members know that you need their help and ask what they are willing or able to do. Don't assume anything.

If there is a gatekeeper blocking you from the senior, attempt to visit and help out. If you are unable to visit in person, you can still send your senior letters and emails, letting them know you care about them.

TAKING CARE OF SENIOR PARENTS WHILE TAKING CARE OF CHILDREN AT HOME

- Can you financially support your family and your parents at the same time? If not, who can you involve to help?

- Is there physically enough room in your house for your family and your parents to live? Do you have the option of moving to a larger home or adding on to your existing home?

- How will your senior parents integrate with your children? How will you handle disagreements?

- How will you manage your time so that you can be with your spouse, children, and parents and still have time by yourself?

FEELING GUILTY FOR PUTTING YOUR PARENTS IN SENIOR LIVING FACILITIES

- What is best for your senior?

- Are you doing everything you can to make sure they are in the best facility possible?

- How can you still be involved with your senior and make them feel loved while they are living in a senior housing facility?

EACH SIBLING SEES THE SENIOR'S NEEDS DIFFERENTLY

- Who is the senior's primary decision maker? Is everyone aware of who this is?

- Are all the adult children part of the planning process? Have you considered everyone's concerns before putting your plan together?

THE SENIOR WON'T ADMIT THAT THEY NEED HELP

- Have you explained your concerns to your senior?

- Have other children and family members expressed their concerns for their senior?

- Are your concerns perceived as *bossy* or *caring*?

- Have you asked your senior why they do not feel the same way you do?

- Is your senior still of sound mind? If not, have you contacted your attorney to investigate the guardianship process?

PAYING FOR SENIOR CARE

- Will all family members contribute to the costs?

- Is one family member the main decision maker for financial matters?

- Have you consulted with your financial advisor?

- Have you contacted local churches and non-profits about free or reduced services for seniors?

- Does your senior qualify for government benefits?

CARING FOR BOTH PARENTS AT THE SAME TIME

- Do you have enough financial, emotional, and physical strength to take care of both parents?

- What are the different needs of each parent?

- Can another family member move in or stop by regularly to help you take care of both parents?

CHAPTER GOAL

The goal of this chapter is to address some concerns that the family members of seniors may have. Be sure to review these questions with your senior and your advisory team.

Hopefully, through an open conversation, you can discover any hidden plan disruptors and move toward a great outcome for your family.

In Closing

We hope that you have received a great deal of value from this book. Even one tip can make a huge difference in the outcome for your senior. Feel free to reach out to us if we can help you in any way.

To find a RAL home near you visit
HTTPS://RALNA.ORG/FIND-A-HOME/

About Gene Guarino

Gene Guarino is the Founder of the Residential Assisted Living National Association.

With over 40 years of experience in starting, owning and operating businesses and investing in Real Estate, Gene is now focused on just one thing: Residential Assisted Living. His mission is to positively impact 10,000,000 seniors and their families over the next 10 years by providing high quality, safe and affordable housing for seniors.

As President, CEO & Founder of the AL Family group of companies Gene trained and supported tens of thousands of people across the US so they can start, own or operate high quality Residential Assisted Living homes. Whether you are a future resident, the family of a future resident or a RAL home owner, Gene is honored to share his wisdom and experiences to help make your path smoother and less complicated.

References

[1] National Center for Health Statistics," *Centers for Disease Control and Prevention*, 3 May 2017. Retrieved from www.cdc.gov/nchs/fastats/life-expectancy.html

[2] "Residential Care, Such as Assisted Living, Memory Care, & Nursing Homes for Persons with Dementia," *Dementia Care Central*, 19 September 2018. Retrieved from www.dementiacarecentral.com/memory-care-vs-assisted-living/

[3] Residential Care, Such as Assisted Living, Memory Care, & Nursing Homes for Persons with Dementia," *Dementia Care Central*, 19 September 2018. Retrieved from www.dementiacarecentral.com/memory-care-vs-assisted-living/

[4] "Aging & Health A to Z." *Health in Aging*. Retrieved from www.healthinaging.org/aging-and-health-a-toz/topic:nursing-homes/

[5] Bernal, N. "Skilled Nursing Care: Fact vs. Myth," *Care Conversations*, 29 October 2014. Retrieved from care-conversations.org/skilled-nursing-care-fact-vs-myth

[6] "CCRC vs Rental Retirement Community | MyLifeSite Blog," *MyLifeSite*, 2 July 2018. Retrieved from www.mylifesite.net/blog/post/ccrc-vs-rental-retirement-community-what-are-the-differences/

[7] "From Family Caregiving to Retirement Communities," *AARP*. Retrieved from www.aarp.org/caregiving/basics/info-2017/continuing-care-retirement-communities.html

[8] "Independent Living Community Price Ranges and Costs," *Brookdale Senior Living Solutions*. Retrieved from www.brookdale.com/en/ where-to-begin/financialconsiderations/independent-living-price-range.html

[9] "Cost of Care," The 2018 Cost of Care Report, *Genworth*. Retrieved from www.genworth.com/aging-and-you/ finances/cost-of-care.html

[10] "So I'll Probably Need Long-Term Care, But for How Long? *MyLifeSite*, 28 June 2018. Retrieved from www.mylifesite. net/blog/post/so-ill-probably-need-long-term-care-but-for-how-long/

[11] Fried, C. "Continuing Care Retirement Community: Can You Afford It?" *Time*, 22 December 2016. Retrieved from time.com/money/4579934/continuing-care-retirement-communities-cost/

[12] Fried, C. "Continuing Care Retirement Community: Can You Afford It?" *Time*, 22 December 2016. Retrieved from time.com/money/4579934/continuing-care-retirement-communities-cost/

[13] "What Is the Current Medicare Coverage for Long-Term Care?" *AARP*. Retrieved from www.aarp.org/health/medicare-qa-tool/current-long-term-nursing-home-coverage/

[14] "Medicare Supplemental Insurance Benefits for Assisted Living & Long-Term Care," *Medicare Supplemental Insurance (Medigap) Benefits for Long-Term Care.* Retrieved from www.payingforseniorcare.com/longterm-care/resources/medigap.html

[15] "Nursing Facilities," *Medicaid.gov.* Retrieved from www.medicaid. gov/medicaid/ltss/institutional/nursing/index.html

[16] "14 Important Reverse Mortgage Facts," *New Retirement,* 12 January 2016. Retrieved from www.newretirement.com/ retirement/14-important-reverse-mortgage-facts/

[17] McKim, J. "More Seniors Are Taking Loans against Their Homes – And It's Costing Them," *The Washington Post,* 25 August 2017. Retrieved from www.washingtonpost.com/business/ economy/more-seniors-are-taking-loans-against-their-homes--and-its-costing-them/2017/08/25/5f154072-883a-11e7-961d-2f373b3977ee_story.html?utm_term=.831aa69 a5b55

[18] Stark, Ellen. "5 Facts You Should Know About Long-Term Care Insurance." *AARP,* 1 Mar. 2018, www.aarp.org/caregiving/financial-legal/info-2018/long-term-care-insurance-fd.html.

[19] Marquand, Barbara. "Long-Term Care Insurance Explained." *NerdWallet,* 28 May 2019, www.nerdwallet.com/blog/insurance/long-term-care-insurance/.

[20] Vogel, Lisa. "Long-Term Care Insurance: How to Use a Policy and File a Claim." *AgingCare.com*, 17 July 2020, www.agingcare.com/articles/how-to-use-a-long-term-care-insurance-policy-198336.htm.

[21] Comfort, Bill. "Navigating Long-Term Care Insurance ." *Long Term Care Guide*, 2018, www.caregiver-stress.com/wp-content/uploads/2018/05/Long-term-care-guide.pdf.

[22] "So I'll Probably Need Long-Term Care, But for How Long? *MyLifeSite*, 28 June 2018. Retrieved from www.mylifesite.net/blog/post/so-ill-probably-need-long-term-care-but-for-how-long/

[23] Frankel, M. "9 Baby-Boomer Statistics That Will Blow You Away," *The Motley Fool*, 29 July 2017. Retrieved from www.fool.com/retirement/2017/07/29/9-baby-boomer-statistics-that-will-blow-you-away.aspx

[24] Gleckman, H. "Who Owns Long-Term Care Insurance?" *Forbes*, 18 August 2016, www.forbes.com/sites/howardgleckman/ 2016/08/18/who-owns-long-term-care insurance/#121f9d6f 2f05

[25] "6 Best Ways to Stimulate Memories through Photos," *Alzheimers.net,* 6 October 2014. Retrieved from www.alzheimers.net/10-6-14-memories-photos

[26] "PACE," *Medicare*. Retrieved from www.medicare.gov/your-medicare-costs/get-help-paying-costs/pace

[27] "Aging," *United Way Worldwide*. Retrieved from www.unitedway.org/our-impact/featured-programs/aging

Made in the USA
Coppell, TX
27 February 2021